The
Ultimate
Book of
Blonde
Brunette
and
Redhead
Jokes

The Ultimate Book of Blonde Brunette and Redhead Jokes

JAMES BUFFINGTON

Ulysses Press

Published in the United States by
ULYSSES PRESS
P.O. Box 3440
Berkeley, CA 94703
www.ulyssespress.com

Printed in the United States by Bang Printing

10 9 8 7 6 5 4 3 2 1

ISBN13: 978-1-56975-793-2
Library of Congress Control Number: 2009943779

Acquisitions Editor: Keith Riegert
Managing Editor: Claire Chun
Editor: Anna Dizon
Front cover design: Double R Design
Back cover design: what!design @ whatweb.com
Cover illustration: John M. Duggan
Proofreader: Alice Riegert
Production: Judith Metzener

Distributed by Publishers Group West

Table of Contents

Blonde
Jokes

How many blondes does it take to make popcorn?
Three. One to hold the pot and two to shake the stove.

＊ ＊ ＊

Why couldn't the blonde call 911?
She couldn't find 11 on the phone.

＊ ＊ ＊

How did the blonde skydiver die?
She missed the earth.

＊ ＊ ＊

What did the blonde do with her first fifty-cent piece?
Married him.

＊ ＊ ＊

Why did the blonde snort NutraSweet?
She thought it was diet coke.

＊ ＊ ＊

What happens when a blonde puts her panties on backwards?
She gets her ass chewed out.

* * *

What did the lesbian blondes do at lunch?
They had a box lunch.

* * *

Did you hear about the blonde bank robber?
She tied up the safe and blew the manager.

* * *

How come blondes don't like gang bangs?
Too many thank-you notes.

* * *

A traveling salesman gets on his flight back home. A beautiful blonde boards shortly after and, to his great delight takes the seat next to him. Not one to pass up an opportunity, the salesman starts a conversation.

"So, Miss, where are you heading?" he asks.

The blonde replies, "I'm going to the nymphomaniacs' convention in Cleveland."

"Really? What are you going to do there?"

"Well," explains the blonde, "we want to dispel some of the myths about sexuality."

"Like what?"

"One myth is that blacks have the biggest cocks. Actually, it's Native Americans. Also, people think the French are the best lovers when it's the Jewish men who really know how to please a woman." She reflected for a minute, then continued. "I'm sorry, but I feel awkward talking about this with you when I don't even know your name."

"Goldberg. Tonto Goldberg."

✳ ✳ ✳

How did the blonde pass her biology exam?
She gave her body to science.

✳ ✳ ✳

What did the blonde do when her boss gave her the pink slip?
She wore it.

* * *

Why did the blonde stand in front of the mirror with her eyes closed?
She wanted to see what she looked like when she's sleeping.

* * *

What do you call a blonde with a running nose?
Full.

* * *

What do you call 144 blondes in the same room?
Gross stupidity.

* * *

What do you call a blonde who's had a lobotomy?
Gifted.

* * *

Then there was the blonde who watched
Sixty Minutes.
It took her an hour and a half.

* * *

How do blonde brain cells die?
Alone.

* * *

A blonde was complaining to a friend about her
boyfriend.
"He has the worst dandruff," she lamented.
"Have you tried giving him Head & Shoulders?"
"How do you give shoulders?"

* * *

What's the difference between a blonde and a
savings bond?
Bonds mature.

* * *

What's the difference between a blonde and a gigolo?
A gigolo can only screw one person at a time.

✳ ✳ ✳

What's the difference between a blonde and the *Titanic*?
Only 500 men went down on the Titanic.

✳ ✳ ✳

What did the blonde senator say when asked about the abortion bill?
"Go ahead and pay it."

✳ ✳ ✳

What's the smartest thing to ever come out of a blonde's mouth?
Albert Einstein.

✳ ✳ ✳

What did the blonde say to her husband when she was feeling sexy?
"Send the kids outside to p-l-a-y so we can fuck."

✳ ✳ ✳

What do you call a blonde with an IQ of fifty?
Your Honor.

✳ ✳ ✳

Why did the man really love his blonde girlfriend?
She had the cutest smile he ever came across.

✳ ✳ ✳

How do you know a blonde really likes you?
You stick her hand in her pants and it feels like a horse feeding.

✳ ✳ ✳

How do you know a blonde is really in love?
She divorces her husband.

✳ ✳ ✳

What's the difference between a blonde and a toilet?
A toilet doesn't want to cuddle after you drop a load into it.

* * *

How did the blonde burn her pussy?
She forgot to blow out the candle.

* * *

Why did God create orgasms?
So blondes would know when to stop screwing.

* * *

What's a blonde's favorite wine?
I want to go to Hawaii!

* * *

Then there was the blonde biker chick who tried to trade her menstrual cycle for a Harley.

* * *

. . . And the blonde who said she'd do anything for a fur coat and now can't button it over her belly.

* * *

. . . Or the blonde who thought Moby Dick was an STD.

* * *

Why don't blondes use ice cubes?
They keep forgetting the recipe.

* * *

Why did the blonde keep her empty beer bottles?
To serve friends who don't drink.

* * *

Why don't blondes breast-feed their babies?
It hurts too much to boil the nipples.

* * *

Then there was the blonde who wanted to become a hooker.
She went to work in a warehouse.

❋ ❋ ❋

How can a man tell when a blonde has an orgasm?
Who cares?

❋ ❋ ❋

What do you call a blonde who can suck a golf ball through a hose?
"Darling!"

❋ ❋ ❋

Why do blondes have two holes so close together?
In case you miss.

❋ ❋ ❋

Why did the blonde want a test tube baby?
So he could have a womb with a view.

❋ ❋ ❋

What's the difference between a blonde and a toilet?
Toilets don't follow you around for weeks when you're through using them.

✳ ✳ ✳

How do you make a blonde laugh on Friday?
Tell her a joke on Monday.

✳ ✳ ✳

Why did the blonde serve curry and baked beans?
She loved Indian music.

✳ ✳ ✳

Why did the blonde stick her boyfriend's cock in her ear?
She wanted to try aural sex.

✳ ✳ ✳

Why did the blonde rush to the department store?
She heard that men's pants were half-off.

✳ ✳ ✳

What did the blonde call her pet zebra?
Spot.

✳ ✳ ✳

How can you tell the blonde in a casino?
She's playing the stamp machine.

✳ ✳ ✳

Then there was the blonde counterfeiter.
She erased the zeros from fifties.

✳ ✳ ✳

How is a blonde's hair like her boyfriend?
They both get blown dry every day.

✳ ✳ ✳

How is a blonde like a Tootsie Pop?
They're both great suckers.

✳ ✳ ✳

What did the blonde do to bring her golfer husband luck?
She licked his balls.

✳ ✳ ✳

A blonde lay in the hospital bed, recuperating from an operation, when her doctor came by to check on her.

"Doctor," she asked, "how soon until I can have sex again?"

"I'm not sure," replied the doctor. "No one's ever asked me that after a tonsillectomy before."

✳ ✳ ✳

Then there was the blonde who's had more fingerprints than the FBI.

✳ ✳ ✳

How can you tell if a blonde has AIDS or Alzheimer's disease?
Take her out in the woods. If she makes it back, don't fuck her.

* * *

Why did the blonde dash to the courthouse?
She heard they had a hung jury.

* * *

Why is a blonde like a doorknob?
Everybody gets a turn.

* * *

What's the hardest thing for a blonde to do on her wedding night?
Say "Ouch!" like she means it.

* * *

What question does a blonde interested in safe sex ask?
"What time will your wife be home?"

* * *

Where does a blonde write her diary?
In a loose-life notebook.

❋ ❋ ❋

Why is a blonde like the Panama Canal?
They're both busy ditches.

❋ ❋ ❋

The blonde played hooky on her correspondence course.
She mailed in empty envelopes.

❋ ❋ ❋

Why did the blonde buy a nightgown with fur around the hemline?
To keep her neck warm.

❋ ❋ ❋

How did the blonde become head cheerleader?
She took an oral exam.

❋ ❋ ❋

Then there was the blonde who made love cafeteria style.
Everybody helps themselves.

* * *

Why did the blonde love being a stockbroker?
She made sure every client got a share.

* * *

Then there was the blonde hooker who went to work on an Indian reservation.
Her first night she made a hundred bucks.

* * *

What happens when you take a blonde sailing and a storm comes up?
You get blown ashore.

* * *

Why is a blonde like a plumber?
They both do a good job cleaning your pipes.

✳ ✳ ✳

Why is a blonde like a front door?
Both have mail slots.

✳ ✳ ✳

What's the toughest part of being a blonde hooker?
You can't whistle while you work.

✳ ✳ ✳

What's the best way to attract blondes at a nudist colony?
Carry two drinks and twelve doughnuts.

✳ ✳ ✳

What did the blonde do with 365 used rubbers?
She made them into a tire and called it a good year.

✳ ✳ ✳

A guy walks into a gift shop and asks the blonde clerk, "Do you keep stationary?"

"Yes," she replied, "Right up until the end. Then I go all to pieces."

✳ ✳ ✳

A blonde walks into a hardware store and asks the clerk if he can help fix a broken lock. "Do you want a screw for the lock?" he asks.

"No, but I'll blow you for a toaster."

✳ ✳ ✳

Why is sex with a blonde like Jell-O?
There's always room for more.

✳ ✳ ✳

Brunette: "Do you make friends quickly?"
Blonde: "Yes, but strangers take a little longer."

✳ ✳ ✳

Then there was the blonde who had a car accident.
She got pregnant.

* * *

Then there was the blonde lesbian.
She picked up men.

* * *

Why are blondes like postage stamps?
They both get sticky when you lick them.

* * *

Why are blondes popular in church?
They're so good at playing the organ.

* * *

Then there was the blonde who wanted to be a
Hollywood star.
She fucked the studio custodian.

* * *

What are the worst six years of a blonde's life?
The third grade.

* * *

Why don't blondes vote?
They don't care who gets in.

* * *

Why did the blonde date a midget?
She wanted to blow a little dope.

* * *

How is a blonde like a Mac?
They're both user-friendly.

* * *

Why do blondes love jellybeans?
They come in so many tasty flavors.

* * *

How do you make a blonde pregnant?
Fuck her.

* * *

Why did the blonde put ice cream on her pussy?
So her boyfriend could have hair pie à la mode.

* * *

What's a blonde's favorite science fiction film?
Close Encounters with the Third Grade.

* * *

What's the difference between a blonde and a
limousine?
Not everyone has been in a limousine.

* * *

Then there were the blonde twins who kept
forgetting each other's birthday.

* * *

Then there was the blonde Olympian who had her
gold medal bronzed.

* * *

How is a blonde genius like raw hamburger?
They are both very rare.

* * *

Why did the blonde stick a lit candle in her pussy?
So her boyfriend could dine by candlelight.

* * *

Two blondes are walking in the woods. "Look!
There's a dead bird!" says one.
    The other looks up.

* * *

How is a blonde like a nail?
Both get hammered.

* * *

Then there was the blonde who was so popular she
kept a change-maker in her pantyhose.

* * *

A little six-year-old blonde girl runs into the house.

"Mommy, can a six-year-old get pregnant?"

"No. Of course not."

The little girl runs back out, calling, "OK, boys! Same game!"

✳ ✳ ✳

Why did the blonde keep failing her driving test?
She couldn't learn to sit up straight in the car.

✳ ✳ ✳

Then there was the blonde who went on a fishing trip with ten men.
She came home with a red snapper.

✳ ✳ ✳

Why won't a blonde ever win the Indianapolis 500?
She'd have to keep stopping to ask for directions.

✳ ✳ ✳

A businessman asked his blonde mistress, "What would you do if you found yourself pregnant and abandoned?"

"I think I'd kill myself."

"Good girl!"

* * *

Then there was the blonde who tried to rob a lawyer.
She lost $2000.

* * *

Why do blondes get only thirty minutes for lunch?
Any longer and they'd have to retrain.

* * *

What does a blonde say when she wants oral sex?
"This bud's for you!"

* * *

Two women were attending the funeral of their blonde friend.

"They're together at last," said the first.

"You mean her and her husband?"

"No, I mean her legs."

* * *

How can you tell a pregnant blonde is going to have a boy?

She's smiling all the time. A blonde is always happy with a dick inside her.

* * *

Why is a sun-tanned blonde like a turkey?

The white meat is best.

* * *

Why did the blonde go to the Halloween party wearing nothing but a lemon over her cunt?

She was a sourpuss.

* * *

Why did eighteen blondes go to the movies together?
The sign said: "Under seventeen not admitted."

* * *

How can you tell a blonde is half Irish and half Italian?
She mashes potatoes with her feet.

* * *

Why did the pregnant blonde have a blood test?
To make sure the baby was really hers.

* * *

How many blondes does it take to make chocolate-chip cookies?
Twenty. One to make the dough, nineteen to peel the M&Ms.

* * *

What does a blonde play on her iPod?
"Left, right, left, right, left, right."

* * *

Why did the blonde stick her head in the freezer?
She wanted to frost her hair.

* * *

Why did the blonde grandmother have a
hysterectomy?
She didn't want any more grandchildren.

* * *

Why did the blonde sell her water skis?
She couldn't find a lake on a hill.

* * *

Why did the blonde take the used tampon to
the museum?
She wanted to see what period it was from.

* * *

Why did the blonde plant Cheerios in her garden?
She thought they were doughnut seeds.

* * *

How did the blonde bruise the side of her head?
She tried to play the piano by ear.

* * *

Did you hear about the blonde plastic surgeon?
She repaired Tupperware.

* * *

What's the first thing a blonde does every morning?
Gets up and drives home.

* * *

Why didn't the blonde know how she got an STD?
She didn't have eyes in the back of her head.

* * *

How do you keep a blonde from leaving her
secretarial job?
Screw her on the desk.

✳ ✳ ✳

Why are blondes so relentless?
They're attireless workers.

✳ ✳ ✳

Why did the blonde blow the snow man?
She loved ice cream.

✳ ✳ ✳

Why don't blondes go to Mt. Rushmore?
They can't decide what face to sit on.

✳ ✳ ✳

What's unique about a blonde's anatomy?
No private parts.

✳ ✳ ✳

What's the difference between a blonde and the
Queen Mary?
It takes a few tugs to get the Queen Mary *out of
her slip.*

* * *

Why did the blonde leave her clothes on the floor
when she came home drunk?
She was in them.

* * *

What does a blonde do with a dog with no legs?
She takes it for a spin.

* * *

Why can't blondes play the outfield?
They drop every fly they get under.

* * *

What's the definition of a lousy party?
Only ten guys to every blonde.

* * *

Why do politicians recruit blondes?
They need enthusiastic pole workers.

* * *

What is a blonde's favorite charity?
The sex drive.

* * *

Why are golden showers with blondes no fun?
She won't come until you go.

* * *

Why do blondes have T.G.I.F. printed on their
T-shirts?
Tits Go In Front.

* * *

Why are there no blonde pharmacists?
They can't fit those tiny bottles in a typewriter.

* * *

What's the first thing a blonde does after sucking
a cock?
Spits out the feathers.

* * *

Why do blondes hate vibrators?
They chip teeth.

* * *

The boss asks his blonde secretary, "Do you know the difference between oral sex and a Caesar salad?"
    "No, boss, I don't."
    "Great! Let's do lunch."

* * *

Why do blondes make great astronauts?
They take up space at school.

* * *

The blonde couple asked their son what he wanted for his birthday.
    "I wanna watch," he replied.
    So they let him.

* * *

What do you call a tie breaker at a blonde beauty pageant?
A fuckoff.

* * *

Why didn't the blonde want her husband shooting craps?
She didn't know how to cook them.

* * *

How did the blonde break her arm raking leaves?
She fell out of the tree.

* * *

Why do blondes wear hats?
So they know which end to wipe.

* * *

Why don't blondes like twelve-inch cocks.
They are afraid of foot-in-mouth disease.

* * *

Why do blondes like penises and Rubik's Cubes?
The more you play with them, the harder they get.

* * *

Then there was the blonde couple into S&M.
He snores, she masturbates.

* * *

There's a new car insurance policy for blondes.
It's called "My Fault."

* * *

A blonde was baking cookies and accidentally started a fire. Immediately, she called the fire department. "Hurry, please or my house will burn down!" she pleaded.

"How do we get there?" asked the operator.

"Don't you guys still have those red trucks?"

* * *

Why do blondes like cars with sunroofs?
More leg room.

* * *

What's the difference between a parrot and a blonde?
Parrots can say "No."

* * *

There's a new lottery for blondes.
Winner gets a dollar a year for a million years.

* * *

What do you put at the top of a blonde's ladder?
"Stop!"

* * *

What does a blonde do when she runs out of sick days?
She calls in dead.

* * *

How is a blonde's IQ like her bra?
They're the same size.

* * *

Why did the blonde stare at the orange juice carton?
The carton said, "Concentrate."

* * *

What's a blonde's favorite game?
Playing dumb.

* * *

Did you hear about the blonde abortion clinic?
There's a twelve-month wait.

* * *

What do you call a blonde in a freezer?
Frosted Flakes.

* * *

Why was the blonde disappointed when she got to London?
She found out Big Ben is a clock.

* * *

What do you call a smart blonde?
A golden retriever.

* * *

A blonde waitress had a pain in her pussy and rushed to her gynecologist. He examined her and said, "This is very strange, but you have a tea bag in your vagina."

"Hmm. I wonder what I served that last customer?"

* * *

How do you brainwash a blonde?
Give her an enema.

* * *

A teenage blonde discovers she's pregnant. "Who did this to you?" demanded her mother.

"How should I know?" replied the teenager. "You never let me go steady!"

* * *

Why are blondes so quiet when they fuck?
They don't talk to strangers.

* * *

Why do blondes wear underwear?
To keep their ankles warm.

* * *

What does a blonde say after sex?
"All you guys on the same team?"

* * *

What do blondes and linoleum have in common?
Lay 'em right the first time and you can walk all over them forever.

* * *

Then there was the blonde midget who went into a bar and kissed everyone in the joint.

* * *

How did the blonde freeze to death?
She went to the drive-in to see, "Closed for the Winter."

* * *

Why don't blondes eat bananas?
They can't find the zipper.

* * *

Why don't blondes eat pickles?
They can't fit their head in the jar.

* * *

Why don't blondes talk to themselves?
Too many stupid answers.

* * *

A blonde asks her son what he wants for his birthday.
"I want an ant farm," he replied.

"Don't be silly," said the blonde mom. "You don't want that."

"Why not?"

"Where are you going to get a tractor that small?"

* * *

Why do blondes lose so much when they gamble?
They bet on instant replays.

* * *

What are a blonde's two biggest lies?

"Your check is in my mouth."

"I promise not to come in the mail."

* * *

Why do blondes like hamburgers?
Hot meat between two buns.

* * *

Why did the blonde think her abortion was illegal?
Because her doctor was wearing a mask.

* * *

What do you call twelve blondes sitting in a circle?
A dope ring.

* * *

Why did the blonde take a box of condoms to school?
They were studying the Trojan War.

* * *

Why did the blonde fuck a robot?
She wanted to be artificially inseminated.

* * *

Why did the blonde's coffee taste like mud?
She used fresh ground every day.

* * *

Why can't blondes teach dogs tricks?
You have to be smarter than the dog.

* * *

What's the definition of eternity?
Four blondes playing "Trivial Pursuit."

* * *

Why couldn't the blonde get security clearance?
She had loose lips.

* * *

What do most executives think the most appropriate
position for a blonde secretary is?
On her back.

* * *

What do you call a blonde clone?
A clunt.

* * *

Why do blondes make lousy race car drivers?
All they care about are their pole positions.

✳ ✳ ✳

What happens when a blonde looks for trouble?
She gets a bellyful.

✳ ✳ ✳

How did the blonde become a cheerleader?
She made the team.

✳ ✳ ✳

Why did the blonde take a sex education class?
She was studying for a better-paying position.

✳ ✳ ✳

How does a blonde teach a dog to fetch?
She ties a cat to a stick and throws it.

✳ ✳ ✳

Why did the blonde hold the letter to her ear?
She thought she had voice mail.

✳ ✳ ✳

Why did the blonde stop using her toilet brush?
Paper doesn't scratch.

* * *

How do you measure a blonde's intelligence?
Put a tire gauge to her ear.

* * *

How do you know a blonde likes you?
She screws you two nights in a row.

* * *

Why are coffins for blondes Y-shaped?
When you lay them on their backs their legs spring apart.

* * *

Why do blondes get confused in the ladies' room?
They have to pull their own pants down.

* * *

What's the mating call of a blonde?
"I'm sooooo drunk!"

* * *

What's the mating call of a really ugly blonde?
"I said, I'm sooooo drunk!"

* * *

Why did the blonde clap her hands to her ears?
She was trying to hold a thought.

* * *

What's the difference between a blonde and a
phone booth?
You need a quarter to use a phone booth.

* * *

Why did God make blondes smarter than horses?
So they wouldn't shit in the street.

* * *

What does a blonde like to do in the morning after a night of hot sex?
Watch the sunrise through the windshield.

* * *

How does a blonde turn on the light after sex?
She opens the car door.

* * *

How do you make a blonde's eyes twinkle?
Shine a flashlight in her ear.

* * *

What can a blonde put in the air to get pregnant?
Her legs.

* * *

Why do blondes hate M&Ms?
They're too hard to peel.

* * *

Why did the blonde get fired from the M&M factory?
For throwing out the Ws.

* * *

Why don't blondes make Kool Aid?
They can't get two quarts of water in those little packages.

* * *

What does a blonde say after multiple orgasms?
"Way to go, team!"

* * *

How do you keep a blonde busy?
Write "see other side" on both sides of a piece of paper.

* * *

How did the blonde die drinking milk?
The cow fell on her.

* * *

How do you know a blonde has been using your computer?
The whiteout on the screen.

* * *

Why do blondes like smart men?
Opposites attract.

* * *

How can you tell a blonde is sexually aroused?
She's breathing.

* * *

What do blondes and beer bottles have in common?
They're both empty from the neck up.

* * *

Why did the blonde refuse to become a Jehovah's Witness?
She didn't see the accident.

✳ ✳ ✳

Why did the blonde take two hits of LSD?
She wanted to go on a round trip.

✳ ✳ ✳

Then there was the blonde who got a degree in psychology so she could blow your mind.

✳ ✳ ✳

A blonde goes into the bank to deposit a hundred dollars. The teller examines the bill and says, "I'm sorry, Miss, but this bill is counterfeit."

"Oh, my God!" cried the blonde. "I've been raped!"

✳ ✳ ✳

Why did the blonde become a nun?
So she could freeze holy water and sell it as Popesicles.

✳ ✳ ✳

Why are guys smart and blondes talkative?
Guys have two heads and blondes have four lips.

* * *

Then there was the blonde who was afraid of
flies . . .
Until she opened one.

* * *

What do you give a blonde on her birthday?
Layered cake.

* * *

Why do so many blondes miss the first day of
school?
Morning sickness.

* * *

Then there was the blonde cheerleader who caught
a case of athlete's fetus.

* * *

Why did the blonde cremate her dead husband?
She wanted a piece of ash.

✳ ✳ ✳

A brunette was talking to her blonde friend about becoming a hooker. "I wonder how long dicks should be sucked?" the brunette pondered.

"Long dicks should be sucked the same as short ones," replied the blonde.

✳ ✳ ✳

A blonde and a redhead go to the beach.

"Don't bother with that suntan oil," says the blonde. "It's worthless."

"How do you know?" asks the redhead.

"I've drunk three bottles and I'm still white as a sheet."

✳ ✳ ✳

Why did the blonde go to the dentist?
She wanted wisdom teeth put in.

✳ ✳ ✳

A blonde and a brunette were talking.

"I found a condom on the patio last night," said the brunette.

"What's a patio?" the blonde replied.

* * *

A blonde got a job as a bartender. Her first night, a customer walks up and asks, "Can you make a martini?"

"Sure," replied the blonde, "but I don't usually date Italian guys."

* * *

A blonde was filling out a job application. Under "Last Position," she wrote "Doggie style."

* * *

Blondes are like computers.
You don't appreciate them until they go down on you.

* * *

An angry blonde goes in to see her gynecologist and rants, "Ever since you fitted me with that diaphragm, I've been pissing purple!"

"That's strange," says the doctor. "What kind of jelly are you using?"

"Grape."

* * *

Then there was the blonde wife who bought a Spanish-American dictionary because she heard every third child born in America is Hispanic.

* * *

Why did the blonde hemophiliac die so young?
Acupuncture.

* * *

What happens when a blonde gets Alzheimer's disease?
Her IQ goes up ten points.

* * *

How do you drown a blonde?
Tell her not to swallow.

✳ ✳ ✳

What is a blonde's favorite game?
Swallow the leader.

✳ ✳ ✳

What do you get when you turn three blondes upside down?
Three brunettes.

✳ ✳ ✳

How do you trick a blonde into marrying you?
Tell her she's pregnant.

✳ ✳ ✳

What do you get when you cross a blonde and a pit bull?
Your last blow job.

✳ ✳ ✳

Then there was the blonde who worked at a sperm bank and got pregnant.
She was arrested for embezzlement.

* * *

How can you tell a burglar is blonde?
She knocks first.

* * *

Why did the blonde sell her computer?
It didn't get HBO.

* * *

Why did the blonde collect burned-out light bulbs?
She was building a darkroom.

* * *

How did the blonde get her head cut off?
Feeding bread crumbs to a helicopter.

* * *

How are blondes like microwave ovens?
They get hot really fast and go off in thirty seconds.

* * *

In what month do blondes talk the least?
February.

* * *

Why was the blonde so good at tennis?
She swung both ways.

* * *

Give a blonde an inch and she wants ten.

* * *

Then there was the blonde embezzler.
She ran off with the accounts payable.

* * *

How do blondes spell farm?
E-I-E-I-O.

✳ ✳ ✳

Why did the blonde drag a chain everywhere?
"Have you ever tried to push one?"

✳ ✳ ✳

What has an IQ of 196?
Eight blondes.

✳ ✳ ✳

Then there was the blonde who went ice-fishing.
　She brought back fifty pounds of ice and drowned trying to fry it.

✳ ✳ ✳

Why did the blonde lose her job at the German bar?
She thought Einstein was one beer.

✳ ✳ ✳

How do blondes celebrate Easter?
They dye brown eggs white.

* * *

Why did the blonde lose her job as an elevator operator?
She couldn't learn the route.

* * *

A blonde just invented a new parachute.
It opens on impact.

* * *

Why do blonde dogs have flat noses?
From chasing parked cars.

* * *

Then there was the blonde whose brother had a case of hemorrhoids.
She offered to help him drink it.

* * *

There are two Santa Clauses in a mall. Which one is blonde?
The one with the Easter basket.

* * *

Then there was the blonde that was arrested for public indecency.
She saw a sign that said "Wet Pavement," and she did.

* * *

Then there was the blonde that shot her dog.
She got a phone tip that her husband was screwing her best friend.

* * *

Why are blonde mothers so strong?
From raising dumbbells.

* * *

How does a blonde spell "fun?"
Y-E-S.

* * *

Why did the blonde climb the chainlink fence?
To see what was on the other side.

* * *

What did the blonde's right leg say to her left?
Nothing. They've never met.

* * *

Why did the blonde have bruises around her navel?
Her boyfriend was a blonde, too.

* * *

Why are the Japanese so smart?
Because they're not blonde.

* * *

What does a blonde say when you blow in her ear?
"Thanks for the refill!"

* * *

What does a bleached blonde have in common with a 747?
Black boxes.

✳ ✳ ✳

What do you call a brunette between two blondes?
Interpreter.

✳ ✳ ✳

What do you call it when a blonde dyes her hair brown?
Artificial intelligence.

✳ ✳ ✳

Why do blondes wash their hair in the kitchen sink?
That's where you wash vegetables.

✳ ✳ ✳

How do you give a blonde a brain transplant?
Blow in her ear.

✳ ✳ ✳

A blonde wife went to see her gynecologist.

"We've been trying to have a baby," she explained. "but no matter how hard we try, I can't seem to get pregnant."

"I'm sure we can fix that," said the doctor. "If you'll take off your panties and get up on the table . . .

"Oh, no!" said the blonde. "I want my husband's baby!"

* * *

What do you do when a blonde feminist throws a hand grenade at you?
Pull the pin and throw it back.

* * *

Two blondes were walking in the woods when they came across some tracks.

"Oh look, bear tracks!" exclaimed the first.

"No, I think those are deer tracks."

"Really? I'm sure those are bear tracks."

They were still arguing when the train hit them.

* * *

What's stamped behind a blonde's ear?
Inflate to 30 PSI.

* * *

A smart blonde, a dumb blonde, and Santa Claus are walking down the street and see a twenty-dollar bill. Who picks it up?
The dumb blonde. The other two don't exist.

* * *

Did you hear about the blonde vandal?
She spray-painted graffiti on chainlink fences.

* * *

What did the blonde do when she learned most accidents happen within thirty-five miles of home?
She moved.

* * *

A blonde calls a pizza shop and orders a medium pepperoni.

"So do you want that cut into four pieces or

eight?" asks the clerk.

"You better cut it into four," answered the blonde. "I could never eat eight."

* * *

Why did the blonde pee on her cornflakes?
Her doctor told her she had sugar in her urine.

* * *

Why did they find the blonde unconscious with a dozen bumps on her head?
She tried to hang herself with a rubber band.

* * *

A blonde goes into the drugstore and asks for some deodorant.

"Do you want the ball type?" asks the clerk.

"No, thank you. It's for under the arms."

* * *

Then there was the blonde that bought an AM radio.
It took her a month to figure out she could play it at night.

* * *

What did the blonde put on her postcards when she went on vacation?
"Having a wonderful time! Where am I?"

* * *

Then there was the blonde whose boyfriend said he loved her.
She believed him.

* * *

Then there was the blonde that locked herself out of her car.
It took her two hours to get her family out.

* * *

What is a metallurgist?
*A man who can look at a platinum blonde and tell
if she's virgin metal or common ore.*

＊ ＊ ＊

Then there was the blonde mother who put an ice
pack on her chest to keep the milk fresh.

＊ ＊ ＊

Why did the blonde blow her lover after sex?
She wanted to have her cock and eat it, too.

＊ ＊ ＊

A blonde goes into a bar and asks for a beer.
    "Anheuser-Busch?" asks the bartender.
    "Just fine. And how's your cock?"

＊ ＊ ＊

Why do blondes like tilt steering wheels?
More head room.

＊ ＊ ＊

How do you brainwash a blonde?
Step on her douche bag.

* * *

Why did the blonde buy a baby bottle?
She had triplets.

* * *

What did the blonde do when she had triplets?
She went looking for the three guys.

* * *

Why did the blonde return her new scarf?
It was too tight.

* * *

What do you call a blonde that gives you a hand job on an airplane?
A highjacker.

* * *

How can you tell a blonde is paranoid?
She puts a condom on her vibrator.

* * *

How does a blonde make pineapple upside-down cake?
First she turns the oven over.

* * *

Why did the blonde perch herself in a tree?
She was promoted to branch manager.

* * *

Why did the pregnant blonde in labor go to the supermarket?
She heard they had free delivery.

* * *

Why did the blonde drive around the block thirty-four times?
Her turn signal was stuck.

✳ ✳ ✳

If Tarzan and Jane were blondes, what would Cheetah be?
The smartest of the three.

✳ ✳ ✳

What does a blonde think 7-11 is?
The emergency number.

✳ ✳ ✳

Why did the blonde name her dog "Herpes"?
It wouldn't heel.

✳ ✳ ✳

How do blondes count to ten?
One, two, three, and another, and another...

✳ ✳ ✳

How did the blonde puncture her ear?
Answering the stapler.

* * *

How can you tell the difference between a bleached
blonde and a natural blonde at the airport?
*The bleached blonde doesn't throw bread crumbs
to the helicopters.*

* * *

If you cross a Native American and a blonde, what
do you call the child?
Running Dumb.

* * *

Why did the blonde fail her bar exam?
She thought an antitrust suit was a chastity belt.

* * *

Then there was the blonde skydiver . . .
She missed the Earth.

* * *

Then there was the blonde who failed her mechanic's test because she thought tail assembly was a lesbian orgy.

✳ ✳ ✳

How can you tell which motorcycle belongs to a blonde?
It's the one with the training wheels.

✳ ✳ ✳

And which tricycle does the blonde have?
The one with the kickstand.

✳ ✳ ✳

What's the best thing about marrying a blonde?
You get to use handicapped parking.

✳ ✳ ✳

Why didn't the blonde serve tea to her friends?
She didn't have a T-shirt.

✳ ✳ ✳

What happened when the blonde bought snow tires
for her car?
They melted on the way home.

* * *

Why is a blonde like the U.S. army?
*Both are open to men between eighteen and
thirty-five.*

* * *

Why did the blonde cross the road?
*Who cares? Why the fuck was she out of bed in
the first place?*

* * *

Why do blondes like army sharpshooters?
They're crack shots.

* * *

Where do blondes work?
At the head office.

✳ ✳ ✳

Then there was the blonde who carried on family traditions.
She swallowed in her mother's footsteps.

✳ ✳ ✳

What do you say to a blonde with a headache?
"Don't stand in front of the dart board."

✳ ✳ ✳

What did the x-ray of the blonde's head show?
Nothing.

✳ ✳ ✳

Why did the blonde plant flowers on the top of her head?
She wanted a beauty spot.

✳ ✳ ✳

A guy walks into a restaurant and orders a pizza. Then he asks his blonde waitress, "Will my pizza be long?"

"No, sir," the blonde replied. "It will be round."

* * *

Why did the blonde flunk geometry?
She thought pies are round, not square.

* * *

A guy orders dinner. Soon his waitress, a blonde, brings it to his table.

"Hey!" says the customer. "You've got your thumb on my steak!"

"Well, I didn't want to drop it again!'

* * *

A blonde goes into a diner and studies the menu. When her waiter comes over, she says, "I'll have the burger, please."

"With pleasure," replies the waiter.

"No, I'll just have fries with that."

✳ ✳ ✳

A man in a diner samples his dinner and calls over his blonde waitress. "Miss, I can't tell if this beef or pork."

"You can't taste the difference?"

"No."

"Then why does it matter?"

✳ ✳ ✳

What does a blonde say when introduced?

"Pleased to eat you."

✳ ✳ ✳

Why did the blonde lose her job at the restaurant?

She couldn't fill the saltshakers. Those holes were so small!

✳ ✳ ✳

A guy decides to bring his new blonde girlfriend to a football game. After the game is over, he asks her if she liked the game.

Blonde: "Oh it was great, I loved watching

those men in tight clothes, but there is one thing I don't understand."

Boyfriend: "What did you not understand?"

Blonde: "Well, at the beginning of the game, both teams flipped a quarter to see who would kick first. Then the rest of the game everybody was yelling 'Get the quarter back, get the quarter back, get the quarter back!' So I thought to myself, gosh it's just a quarter!"

* * *

Why do blondes wear green lipstick?
Because red means stop.

* * *

Three blondes are in an elevator when the elevator suddenly stops and the lights go out. They try using their cell phones to get help, but have no luck. Even the phones are out.

After a few hours of being stuck with no help in sight, one blonde says to the others, "I think the best way to call for help is by yelling together."

The others agree with the first, so they all inhale deeply and begin to yell, "Together, together, together!"

✳ ✳ ✳

How can you tell when a blonde is dating?
By the buckle print on her forehead.

✳ ✳ ✳

How can you tell which guy is a blonde's boyfriend?
He's the one with the belt buckle that matches the impression in her forehead.

✳ ✳ ✳

One day, a crowd of blondes met in New York to show the world once and for all that blondes aren't dumb.

As they stood on the street, they challenged the onlookers: "Ask any one of us any question, and we will show you that we're not dumb."

A passerby volunteered to ask them some questions. He climbed up on a car and randomly picked a blonde out of the crowd.

She got up on the car, too, and the man asked: "What is the first month of the year?"

Blonde: "November?"

"Nope," said the man. At this point the other blondes began to chant, "Give her another chance, give her another chance!"

So the man asked: "What is the capital of the United States?"

Blonde: "Los Angeles?"

Man: "Wrong, it's Washington, D.C."

So the crowd of blondes began chanting again: "Give her another chance, give her another chance!"

Man: "OK, but this is the last one. What is one plus one?"

Blonde: "Two?"

"Give her another chance, Give her another chance!" screamed the crowd.

✳ ✳ ✳

What do you call two nuns and a blonde?
Two tight ends and a wide receiver.

✳ ✳ ✳

There was this bar and in the bar there was a magic mirror. If you told a lie it would suck you in.

One day, a brunette walked into the bar. She went up to the mirror and said, "I think I'm the most beautiful woman in the world," and it sucked her in.

The next day, a redhead walked into the bar.

She walked up to the mirror and said, "I think I'm the most beautiful woman in the world," and it sucked her in.

Then the next day, a blonde walked into the bar. She walked up to the mirror and said, "I think . . ." and it sucked her in.

* * *

A blonde goes to work one morning, crying her eyes out. Concerned, her boss walks over to her and asks sympathetically, "What's the matter?"

The blonde replies, "Early this morning, I got a phone call that my mother had passed away."

The boss, feeling very sorry for her suggests, "Why don't you go home for the day? Just take the day off and go relax."

The blonde very calmly states, "No, I'd be better off here. I need to keep my mind busy and I have the best chance of doing that here."

The boss agrees and allows her to work as usual. "If you need anything, just let me know," he says.

A few hours pass and the boss checks on her. When he looks out his office, he sees the blonde crying hysterically. He rushes over and asks, "What's the matter now? Are you going to be OK?"

Through tears, the blonde says, "I just received a horrible call from my sister. She said that her mom died, too!"

* * *

How many blondes does it take to screw in a light bulb?
Two. One to hold the light bulb and one to spin the ladder around.

* * *

A blonde cop stops a blonde motorist and asks for her driver's license.

The motorist fishes around in her purse, but can't find it. She says to the cop, "I must have left it at home, officer."

The cop says, "Well, do you have any kind of identification?" The motorist looks through her purse again and finds a pocket mirror.

She looks at it and says to the cop, "All I have is this picture of myself." The officer says, "Let me see it, then." So the blonde motorist gives the mirror to the blonde cop, who looks at it, and replies, "Well, if I had known you were a police officer, I wouldn't have even pulled you over. You can go now."

* * *

Why did the blonde wear condoms on her ears?
So she wouldn't get hearing AIDS.

* * *

A blonde and a brunette were discussing their boyfriends:

Brunette: Last night I had three orgasms in a row!

Blonde: That's nothing; last night I had over a hundred.

Brunette: My god! I had no idea your boyfriend was that good.

Blonde: Oh, you mean with one guy?

* * *

Why do blondes wear shoulder pads?
(With a rocking of the head from side to side)
I dunno!

* * *

There was a blonde who found herself sitting next to a lawyer on an airplane. The lawyer kept bugging the blonde, wanting her to play a game of intelligence. Finally, the lawyer offered her 10 to 1 odds, and said every time the blonde could not answer one of his questions, she owed him $5, but every time he could not answer hers, he'd give her $50. The lawyer figured he could not lose, and the blonde reluctantly accepted.

The lawyer first asked, "What is the distance between the Earth and the nearest star?"

Without saying a word, the blonde handed him $5. Then the blonde asked, "What goes up a hill with three legs and comes back down the hill with four legs?"

The lawyer looked puzzled. He took several hours, looking up everything he could on his laptop and even placing numerous air-to-ground phone calls trying to find the answer. Finally, angry and frustrated, he gave up and paid the blonde $50.

The blonde put the $50 into her purse without comment, but the lawyer insisted, "What is the answer to your question?"

Without saying a word, the blonde handed him $5.

✳ ✳ ✳

A blonde had just totaled her car in a horrific accident. Miraculously, she managed to pry herself from the wreckage without a scratch and was applying fresh lipstick when the state trooper arrived.

"My God!" the trooper gasped. "Your car looks like an accordion that was stomped on by an elephant. Are you OK, ma'am?"

"Yes, officer, I'm just fine," the blonde chirped.

"Well, how in the world did this happen?" the officer asked as he surveyed the wrecked car.

"Officer, it was the strangest thing!" the blonde began. "I was driving along this road when from out-of-nowhere, this tree pops up in front of me. So I swerved to the right, and there was another tree! I swerved to the left, and there was another tree! I served to the right again, and there was another tree! I swerved to the left again, and there was ...."

"Uh, Ma'am," the officer said, cutting her off. "There isn't a tree on this road for thirty miles. That was your air freshener swinging back and forth."

✳ ✳ ✳

What do you call a blonde between two brunettes? *A mental block.*

* * *

A plane is on its way to Detroit when a pretty blonde in the economy section gets up and moves into an open seat in first class.

The flight attendant watches her do this and politely informs the blonde that she must sit in the economy section because that's the type of ticket she paid for.

The blonde replies, "I'm blonde, I'm beautiful, I'm going to Detroit and I'm staying right here."

After repeated attempts and no success at convincing the woman to move, the flight attendant goes into the cockpit and informs the pilot and co-pilot that there's a blonde sitting in first class who refuses to go back to her proper seat. The co-pilot goes back to the woman and explains why she needs to move, but once again the woman replies by saying, "I'm blonde, I'm beautiful, I'm going to Detroit and I'm staying right here."

The co-pilot returns to the cockpit and suggests that perhaps they should have the arrival gate call the police and have the woman arrested when they land. The pilot says, "You say she's blonde? I'll handle this. I'm married to a blonde. I speak blonde." He goes back to the woman and whispers quietly in her ear, and she says, "Oh, I'm sorry," then quickly moves back to her seat in economy class.

The flight attendant and co-pilot are amazed and ask him what he said to get her to move back to economy without causing any fuss.

"I told her first class isn't going to Detroit."

✳ ✳ ✳

What's the difference between Indiana and a blonde?
A blonde has larger hills and deeper valleys.

✳ ✳ ✳

A young ventriloquist is touring the clubs and one night he's doing a show in a small town in Arkansas. With his dummy on his knee, he starts going through his usual dumb blonde jokes when a blonde in the 4th row stands on her chair and starts shouting: "I've heard enough of your stupid blonde jokes! What makes you think you can stereotype women that way? What does the color of a person's hair have to do with her worth as a human being? It's guys like you who keep women like me from being respected at work and in the community and from reaching our full potential as a person, and all in the name of humor!" The embarrassed ventriloquist begins to apologize, and the blonde yells, "You stay out of this, mister! I'm talking to that little shit on your knee."

∗ ∗ ∗

How does a blonde high-five?
She smacks herself in the forehead.

∗ ∗ ∗

This blonde decides one day that she is sick and tired of all these blonde jokes and how all blondes are perceived as stupid, so she decides to show her husband that blondes really are smart. While her husband is off at work, she decides that she is going to paint a couple of rooms in the house.

The next day, right after her husband leaves for work, she gets down to the task at hand. Her husband arrives home at 5:30 p.m. and smells the distinctive smell of paint. He walks into the living room and finds his wife lying on the floor in a pool of sweat.

He notices that she is wearing a ski jacket and a fur coat at the same time.

He goes over and asks her if she is OK. She says yes. He asks her what she is doing. She replies that she wanted to prove to him that not all blonde women are dumb and she wanted to do it by painting the house. He then asks her why she has a ski jacket over her fur coat. She replies that she was reading the directions on the paint can and it said: FOR BEST RESULTS, PUT ON TWO COATS.

✳ ✳ ✳

Did you hear the one about the blonde who had a bumper sticker that said: "ALL BLONDES AREN'T DUMB?"
No one could read it because it was hung upside down.

✳ ✳ ✳

Why did the blonde nurse take a red magic marker to work?
In case she had to draw some blood.

✳ ✳ ✳

Why does it take longer to build a blonde snowman than a regular one?
You have to hollow out the head.

✳ ✳ ✳

How do you get a blonde to climb on the roof?
Tell her that the drinks are on the house.

✳ ✳ ✳

This blonde walked into a party store and asked the cashier if he had a hanger or something to unlock her car because she locked her keys in the car. He nodded and handed her a hanger. She thanked him and went outside to set to work. A little while later, the cashier decided to check on her and saw her busily working at the lock while another blonde, inside the car, was saying, "a little to the left . . . no, a little to the right . . ."

✳ ✳ ✳

A British Airways employee took a call from a blonde asking the question, "How long is the Concorde flight from London to New York?"

"Um, just a minute, if you please," he murmured. Then, as he turned to check the exact flight time, he heard a polite, "Thank you," as the blonde caller hung up.

✳ ✳ ✳

How do you describe a blonde, surrounded by drooling idiots?
Flattered.

✳ ✳ ✳

Great Blonde Inventions:
1. Tricycle kickstand
2. Solar flashlight
3. Fireproof matches
4. Inflatable dartboard
5. Glass hammer
6. Black light bulb
7. Boomerang grenade

✳ ✳ ✳

What do you call a fly buzzing inside a blonde's head?
A space invader.

＊ ＊ ＊

What's a blonde's favorite rock group?
Air Supply.

＊ ＊ ＊

She was soooooooooooo blonde . . . she:
    Got stabbed in a shoot-out.
    Thought Meow Mix was a record for cats.
    Put lipstick on her forehead because she
        wanted to make up her mind.
    Told me to meet her at the corner of "walk" and
        "don't walk."
    Tried to put M&Ms in alphabetical order.
    Thought a quarterback was a refund.
    Got locked in a grocery store and nearly starved
        to death.
    Tripped over a cordless phone.
    Took a ruler to bed to see how long she slept.
    Asked for a price check at the Dollar Store.
    Tried to drown a fish.
    Studied for a blood test . . . and failed.

Thought Boyz II Men was a daycare center.
Sold the car for gas money.
Called me to get my phone number.
Thought she needed a ticket to get on *Soul Train*.
Sent me a fax with a stamp on it.

＊ ＊ ＊

Did you hear about the blonde?
They had to burn the school down to get her out of third grade.

＊ ＊ ＊

If you gave her a penny for intelligence, you'd get change back.

＊ ＊ ＊

Under "education" on her job application, she put "Hooked On Phonics."

＊ ＊ ＊

At the bottom of the application where it says "sign here," she put "Sagittarius."

* * *

When she missed the 44 bus, she took the 22 bus twice instead.

* * *

When she took you to the airport and saw a sign that said "Airport Left," she turned around and went home.

* * *

If she spoke her mind, she'd probably be speechless.

* * *

Two blondes were driving along a road by a wheat field when they saw another blonde in the middle of the field rowing a boat.

The first blonde turned to her friend and said, "You know, it's blondes like that that give us a bad name!"

To this, the second blonde replied: "Don't I know it, and if I knew how to swim, I'd go out there and drown her."

✳ ✳ ✳

How do you brainwash a blonde?
Give her a douche and shake her upside down.

✳ ✳ ✳

During late spring one year, a blonde was trying out her new boat. She was unable to get her boat to travel through water, or do any maneuvers whatsoever, no matter how hard she tried. After trying for more than three days to make it work properly, she decided to seek help. She took the boat over to the local marina in hopes that someone there could identify her problem.

After a thorough inspection, workers determined that everything was working perfectly on the topside of the boat. So a puzzled marina employee jumped into the water to check underneath the boat for problems. Because he was laughing so hard, he came up choking on water and gasping for air. Under the boat, still strapped in place securely, was the trailer.

✳ ✳ ✳

A blonde, brunette and redhead pass away in a car accident.

When they arrive at the pearly gates, they are informed that they will be told a joke every ten steps, and that they must make it up to 100 steps without laughing. If they laugh before they reach the 100th step, they will not able to get in.

The brunette goes up thirty steps and laughs. The redhead makes it up fifty steps before laughing. The blonde gets all the way to the top, but then starts laughing hysterically.

When asked why she laughed when she got to the top, the blonde replies, "I just got the first joke!"

✳ ✳ ✳

Once upon a time, there was a woman with long blonde hair and blue eyes, who was so sick of all the blonde jokes that she decided to get a makeover. So she cut her hair and dyed it brown. Later that same day, she was driving down a country road and came across a herd of sheep. She stopped and called the sheepherder over.

"That's a nice flock of sheep," she said.

"Thank you," said the herder.

"I have a proposition for you," said the woman.

"OK," replied the herder.

"If I can guess the exact number of sheep in your flock, can I take one home?" asked the woman.

"Sure," said the sheepherder.

So the woman looked at the herd for a second and then replied, "382."

"Wow," said the herder. "That is exactly right. Go ahead and pick out the sheep you want to take home."

So the woman went and picked one, and put it in her car.

Upon watching this, the herder approached the woman and said, "Now I have a proposition for you."

"What is it?" the woman asked.

"If I can guess the real color of your hair, can I have my dog back?"

✳ ✳ ✳

Why are blondes like corn flakes?
Because they're simple, easy, and they taste good.

* * *

A dumb blonde was bragging about her knowledge of the state capitals of the United States. She proudly announced, "Go ahead, ask me any of the capitals, I know all of them."

A redhead said, "OK, what's the capital of Wyoming?"

The blonde replied, "Oh, that's easy, it's 'W.'"

* * *

President Bush and Donald Rumsfeld are sitting in a bar.

A guy walks in and asks the bartender, "Isn't that Bush and Rumsfeld sitting over there?"

The bartender says, "Yep, that's them."

So the guy walks over and says, "Wow, this is a real honor. What are you guys doing in here?"

Bush says, "We're planning WWIII."

And the guy says, "Really? What's going to happen?"

Bush says, "Well, we're going to kill 140 million Iraqis this time and one blonde with big tits."

The guy exclaimed, "A blonde with big tits? Why kill a blonde with big tits?"

Bush turns to Rumsfeld and says, "See, I told you no one would worry about the 140 million Iraqis!"

∗ ∗ ∗

One day, as a blonde was walking along the shore of a huge lake, she spotted another blonde on the opposite shore.

She cupped her hands together and shouted, "How do I get to the other side?"

The other blonde cupped her hands together and shouted "YOU ARE ON THE OTHER SIDE!"

∗ ∗ ∗

Did you hear about the blonde who took an hour to cook Minute Rice?

∗ ∗ ∗

Did you hear about the blonde who got into a taxi, and the driver kept the "Vacant" sign up?

* * *

Did you hear about the blonde who was an M.D.(Mentally Deficient)?

* * *

Did you hear about the blonde who thought nitrates were cheaper than day rates?

* * *

Did you hear about the blonde who, after watching the ballerinas, wondered why they didn't get taller girls?

* * *

Did you hear about the blonde who went to a nudist camp for a game of strip poker?

* * *

Did you hear about the blonde who brought along her cosmetics for a make-up exam?

✳ ✳ ✳

Someone saw a blonde eating a Tootsie Pop and asked her, "So, how many licks does it take to get to the center of a Tootsie Pop?"

Without a thought, the blonde replied, "Beats me, but it took almost the whole day just to lick through the wrapper."

✳ ✳ ✳

A blonde was having financial troubles so she decided to kidnap a child and demand a ransom. She went to a local park, grabbed a little boy, took him behind a tree and wrote this note: "I have kidnapped your child. I am sorry to do this, but I need the money. Leave $10,000 in a plain brown bag behind the big oak tree in the park at 7 a.m." Signed, "The Blonde."

She pinned the note inside the little boy's jacket and told him to go straight home. The next morning, she returned to the park to find the $10,000 in a brown bag behind the big oak tree, just as she had instructed. Inside the bag was the following note: "Here is your money. I cannot believe that one blonde would do this to another."

* * *

What do you call a blonde in an institution of higher learning?
A visitor.

* * *

A blonde was telling her priest a Pollock joke, when halfway through, the priest interrupts her, "Don't you know I'm Polish?"

"Oh, I'm sorry," the blonde apologizes, "do you want me to start over and talk slower?"

* * *

A blonde decided she needed something new and different for a winter hobby. She went to the bookstore and bought every book she could find on ice-fishing.

For weeks she read and studied, hoping to become an expert in the field. Finally, she decided she knew enough and out she went for her first ice-fishing trip. She carefully gathered up and packed all the tools and equipment needed for the excursion.

When she got to the ice, she found a quiet

little area to place her padded stool and carefully laid out her tools. Just as she was about to make her first cut into the ice, a booming voice from the sky bellowed, "There are no fish under the ice!" Startled, the blonde grabbed up all her belongings, moved further along the ice, poured some hot chocolate from her thermos, and started to cut a new hole.

Again the voice from above bellowed, "There are no fish under the ice!"

Amazed, the blonde was not quite sure what to do as this certainly was not covered in any of her books. She packed up her gear and moved to the far side of the ice. Once there, she stopped for a few moments to regain her calm. Then she was extremely careful to set everything up perfectly— tools in the right place, chair positioned just so. Just as she was about to cut this new hole, the voice came again. "There are no fish under the ice!" Petrified, the blonde looked skyward and asked, "Is that you, Lord?" The voice boomed back, "NO, THIS IS THE MANAGER OF THE SKATING RINK!"

✳ ✳ ✳

A blonde hurried into the hospital emergency room

late one night with the tip of her index finger shot off.

"How did this happen?" the emergency room doctor asked her.

"I was trying to commit suicide," the blonde replied.

"What?" sputtered the doctor. "You tried to commit suicide by shooting off the tip of your finger?"

"No, silly!" the blonde said. "First, I put the gun to my chest, and I thought, 'I just paid $6,000 for these; I'm not shooting myself in the chest.'"

"So what then?" asked the doctor.

"Then I put the gun in my mouth, and I thought, 'I just paid $3,000 to get my teeth straightened; I'm not shooting myself in the mouth.'"

"And then?"

"Then I put the gun to my ear, and I thought, 'This is going to make a loud noise,' so I put my finger in the other ear before I pulled the trigger."

✳ ✳ ✳

Three blondes were walking through a burning desert when they found a magic genie's lamp. They rubbed the lamp and soon the genie appeared. "I will grant three wishes, one for each of you," the genie said.

The first blonde quickly said, "I wish I were smarter." Immediately, she was turned into a redhead.

The second blonde said, "I wish I were smarter than she is."

And so she was changed into a brunette.

The third blonde thought a moment, then said, "I wish I were smarter than both of them!"

"It shall be as you request, "the genie said. And with that, she was turned into a man.

✳ ✳ ✳

What is a blonde's favorite part of a gas station?
The air pump.

✳ ✳ ✳

A brunette, a redhead, and a blonde were left alone in jail while the deputy sheriff went out on a lunch break. They soon decided to break out. After finding all the door locked from the outside, the three women managed to escape through an unlocked window. They were pondering what to do next when the brunette had an idea. She said, "Let's hide in that barn, they'll never find us there." So they went into the barn and climbed up the ladder into the hayloft, then threw the ladder down.

The next morning, the sheriff arrived at the barn and said, "Come out with your hands in the air!" The redhead whispered to the blonde and brunette, "Hide in those baskets, they'll never find us!" So the brunette climbed inside the first basket, the redhead went into the second basket, and the blonde got in the third basket. Meanwhile, the sheriff and his men were setting up a ladder. When they reached the hayloft, the sherrif ordered his men to kick the baskets. One of the men kicked the first basket: "RUFF!"

"It's just a damn dog!" yelled the deputy.

Then the deputy kicked the next basket: "MEOW!"

"It's just a damn cat!" yelled the deputy.

Finally, another deputy kicked the last basket and the blonde yelled, "POTATOES!"

✳ ✳ ✳

What's the difference between a blonde and a broom closet?
Only two men fit inside a broom closet at once.

✳ ✳ ✳

One day this blonde was riding a horse. Soon, the blonde decides she wants to go faster and do some tricks so she starts turning the horse around in a circle. All of a sudden, she starts to slip, so she grabs the horse's mane. But even though she has hold of the mane, she's still slipping. So she decides the best thing is to hold on by putting her foot in the saddle. There she is riding along, hanging from her foot, with her head banging on the ground, almost near death, when the WalMart guy comes over and turns off the horse.

✳ ✳ ✳

A government study has shown that blondes do have more fun—they just don't remember who with.

✳ ✳ ✳

There was a blonde named Gayle, who was having serious financial problems. So she got down on her knees and prayed: "Dear God, please let me win the lottery. I really need your help or I'll lose my house, the car, and everything else!"

    She doesn't win, so the next day, she got down on her knees and prayed: "Dear God, I really, really need your help, or I'll lose my house, the car, and everything else!"

Once again she doesn't win. The next day she says the same prayer, then God speaks to her, "Gayle! Work with me here. BUY A TICKET!"

* * *

Why do men like blonde jokes?
Because they can understand them.

* * *

A blonde walks into an electronics store and asks the manager, "Can I buy that TV?"

Manager: "No."

Blonde: "Why not?"

Manager: "Because you're a blonde."

So the blonde goes out and dyes her hair red. She returns to the store and asks, "Can I buy that TV?"

Manager: "No."

Blonde: "Why not?"

Manager: "You're a blonde."

So the blonde goes and shaves off her hair and again returns to the store.

Blonde: "Can I buy that TV?"

Manager: "No."

Blonde: "Why not?"

Manager: "You're a blonde."

Blonde: "How can you tell I'm a blonde? I dyed my hair red, then shaved it off!"

Manager: "Because that's not a TV—that's a microwave!"

＊ ＊ ＊

What does a blonde owl say?

"What, what?"

＊ ＊ ＊

A young blonde was on vacation in the depths of Louisiana.

She wanted a pair of genuine alligator shoes in the worst way, but was very reluctant to pay the high prices the local vendors were asking.

After becoming very frustrated with the "no haggle" attitude of one of the shopkeepers, the blonde shouted, "Maybe I'll just go out and catch my own alligator so I can get a pair of shoes at a reasonable price!"

The shopkeeper said, "By all means, be my guest. Maybe you'll luck out and catch yourself a big one!"

Determined, the blonde turned and headed for the swamps, set on catching herself an alligator.

Later in the day, the shopkeeper was driving home, when he spotted the young woman standing waist deep in the water, shotgun in hand.

Just then, he saw a huge 9-foot alligator swimming quickly toward her. She took aim, killed the creature, and with a great deal of effort hauled it on to the swamp bank.

Lying nearby were several more of the dead creatures. The shopkeeper watched in amazement.

Just then, the blonde flipped the alligator on its back. Frustrated, she shouts out, "Damn it, this one isn't wearing any shoes either!"

✳ ✳ ✳

How do you describe three prostitutes and a blonde?
Ho, Ho, Ho, and to all a good night.

✳ ✳ ✳

A blonde, a brunette, and a redhead were trying out for a new NASA experiment on sending women to different planets. First, they called the brunette in and asked her a question.

"If you could go to any planet, what planet would you want to go to and why?"

After pondering the question, she answered, "I would like to go to Mars because it seems so interesting with all the recent news about possible extraterrestrial life on the planet."

They said, "Well OK, thank you," and told her that they would get back to her.

Next, the redhead entered the room and the NASA agents asked her the same question. She replied, "I would like to go to Saturn to see all of its rings." Again they said, "Thank you" and told her that they would get back to her.

Finally, the blonde entered the room and they asked her the same question they asked the brunette and the redhead. She thought for awhile and then replied, "I would like to go to the sun."

The agents from NASA replied, "Why, don't you know that if you went to the sun you would burn to death?"

The blonde smirked and put her hands on her hips. "Are you guys dumb? I'd go at night!"

✳ ✳ ✳

Why is it okay for blondes to catch cold?
They don't have to worry about blowing their brains out.

* * *

There were three women, a brunette, a redhead, and a blonde. They all worked together at an office. Every day they noticed that their boss left work a little early. So one day, they met for lunch and decided that today when the boss left, they would all leave early, too.

The boss left and so did they. The brunette went home and straight to bed so could get an early start the next morning. The redhead went home to get in a quick workout before her dinner date. The blonde went home and walked into the bedroom. She opened the door slowly and saw her husband in bed with her boss, so she very quietly shut the door and left.

The next day, the brunette and the redhead are talking about going home early again. They ask the blonde if she wants to leave early again, too.

"No," she replies. "Yesterday, I nearly got caught!"

* * *

Why aren't blondes good cattle herders?
Because they can't keep two calves together!

* * *

Two blondes thought they would save money by re-siding their house themselves. After assembling all the necessary materials, the first blonde put on a nail bag and started pounding in nails.

As the second blonde brought over another piece of siding, she watched the first blonde take out a nail, look at it, and then throw it over her shoulder. The next nail she pounded in, but only after looking at it first. The second blonde watched this routine for some time, and finally asked the first blonde why she was throwing some of the nails over her shoulder.

The the first blonde said that when she pulled a nail out from the bag and looked at it, if the point of the nail was facing her, the nail had to be defective!

The second blonde said, "Those nails are not defective. They're for the other side of the house!"

* * *

Why is a blonde like an old washing machine?
They both drip when they're fucked.

* * *

What's a blonde's idea of safe sex?
Locking the car door.

* * *

A blonde was walking down the street with her blouse wide open. The policeman sees her and says, "Excuse me, but do you know your blouse is open?" The blonde screams, "OH MY GOD! I LEFT MY BABY ON THE BUS!"

* * *

A blonde reports for her university final exam, which consists of "yes/no"-type questions. She takes her seat in the examination hall and stares at the exam for five minutes. In a fit of inspiration, she takes out her purse, removes a coin, and starts tossing the coin and marking the answer sheet "Yes" for heads and "No" for tails. Within half-an-hour she is all done, whereas the rest of the class is sweating it out. During the last few minutes, she is seen desperately throwing the coin, uttering and sweating. The moderator, alarmed, approaches her and asks what is going on. "I finished the exam in a half-hour, but I'm re-checking my answers."

✳ ✳ ✳

How can you tell if a blonde writes mysteries?
She has a checkbook.

✳ ✳ ✳

There were three blondes stranded on an island far, far away. They saw a magic bottle floating on the water. They retrieved it, then tried rubbing it to see what would happen. A genie came out and said, "Thank you very much, ladies. Just for that, I will grant each of you one wish and one wish only." So all three blondes were happy.

The first blonde said, "I want to be rich and have a big mansion with a big swimming pool," and POOF! she disappeared and was off having a good time.

The second blonde said, "I want to be a millionaire and own a plane with a cute husband to take care of me and travel the world," and POOF! she was off with her new husband, having a good time.

Then the third blonde looked so sad. The genie

asked, "What is wrong?" The blonde said, "You know what I wish? I wish my friends were back here with me," and POOF! there they all were, back together again.

✳ ✳ ✳

Why do blondes wear their hair up?
To catch everything that goes over their heads.

✳ ✳ ✳

A dumb blonde died and went to heaven. When she got to the Pearly Gates, she met Saint Peter who said, "Before you get to come into heaven, you have to pass a test."

"Oh, no!" she cried, but Saint Peter said not to worry, he'd make it easy.

"Who was God's son?" asked Saint Peter.

The dumb blonde thought for a few minutes and said, "Andy!"

"That's interesting . . . what made you say that?" asked Saint Peter.

Then she started to sing, "Andy walks with me! Andy talks with me! Andy tells me . . . . "

✳ ✳ ✳

What was the blonde psychic's greatest achievement?
An in-body experience!

* * *

Three blondes were witnesses to a crime, so they went to the police station to identify the suspect. The police chief said he would show them a mug shot of someone for thirty seconds, then ask each one for a description. After showing the photo to the first blonde, he covered it, then asked her how she would recognize the suspect.

"Easy," she replied. "He only has one eye."

The chief was stunned. "He only has one eye because it is a profile shot! Think about it!" He repeated the procedure for the second blonde and again asked how she would recognize the suspect.

"He only has one ear," she answered.

"What is the matter with you people? It is a profile shot! You are seeing him from the side!" He repeated the procedure for the third blonde, asking her, "How would you recognize the suspect? Now think before you give me a stupid answer."

After viewing the photo, she thought for a minute, then said, "He's wearing contact lenses."

This took the chief by surprise. He looked real

hard at the picture and couldn't tell if the suspect had contacts or not, so he went into the database and looked at the report. Sure enough, when the mug shot was taken, he was wearing contact lenses! He went back to her and asked, "How could you tell he was wearing contact lenses? Nobody else here in this precinct saw that!"

"Well," she said, "he can't wear regular glasses with only one eye and one ear, now can he?"

* * *

A blonde, a brunette, and a redhead went to their gynecologist for prenatal exams. The doctor asked the brunette: "In what position was the baby conceived?"

"My husband was on top," she replied.

"You will have a boy!" the doctor exclaimed.

The redhead was asked the same question.

"I was on top," was her reply.

"You will have a baby girl," said the doctor.

With this, the blonde burst into tears.

"What's the matter?" asked the doc.

"Does that mean I am going to have puppies?" she cried.

* * *

Why do blondes take the pill?
So they know what day of the week it is.

* * *

Why did the blonde stop using the pill?
Because it kept falling out.

* * *

A middle-aged guy drove his brand new Mercedes to his favorite a local sporting goods store.
He parked it out front and went in to do a little shopping. A pretty blonde sales clerk happily greeted him and said to let her know if he needed any help. But he just wanted to look around on his own, so she obliged and let him do his own thing. However, just five minutes later, the blonde clerk came running up to the man yelling, "Sir! Sir! I just saw someone driving off with your new Mercedes!"

"Dear God! Did you try to stop him?" the stunned man asked.

"No," she said, "I did better than that! I got the license plate number!"

* * *

Why is a blonde like railroad tracks?
Because she's been laid all over the country.

＊ ＊ ＊

A blind guy on a bar stool shouts to the bartender, "Wanna hear a blonde joke?"

In a hushed voice, the guy next to him says, "Before you tell that joke, you should know something. Our bartender is blond and the bouncer is blond. I'm blond, 6' tall, 200 lb. black belt. The guy sitting next to me is blond, 6'2", weighs 225 and he's a rugby player. The fella to your right is also blond, 6'5", pushing 300—and he's a wrestler. Each one of us is a blonde. Think about it, Mister. You still wanna tell that joke?"

The blind guy says, "Nah, not if I'm gonna have to explain it five times."

＊ ＊ ＊

One day, a blonde walked into the doctor's office with two red ears.

The doctor asked what happened. She said, "I was ironing and the phone rang and I picked up the iron by mistake."

"What happened to the other ear?" the doctor asked.

"They called back," she replied.

＊ ＊ ＊

Why can't blondes put in light bulbs?
They keep breaking them with the hammers.

＊ ＊ ＊

A blonde goes to a local restaurant, buys a small drink for herself, and sits down to drink it. She notices a peel-off prize sticker on the side of her cup while she is drinking. After pulling off the tab, she begins screaming, "I won a motor home! I won a motor home!"

The waitress runs over and argues, "That's impossible. The biggest prize given away was a stereo system!"

The blonde replies, "No. I won a motor home!"

By this time, the manager makes his way over to the table, and he, too, argues, "You couldn't possibly have won a motor home because we didn't have that as one of our prizes."

Again the blonde says, "There is no mistake! I won a motor home!"

The blonde hands the prize ticket to the manager and he reads, "WIN A BAGEL."

* * *

What is a cool refreshing drink for a blonde?
Perri-air.

* * *

A blonde bought two horses, but could never remember which horse was which. A neighbor suggested that she cut the tail of one horse, and that worked great until the other horse got his tail caught in a bush. It tore just right and looked exactly like the other horse's tail and the blonde was stuck again.

The neighbor suggested she notch the ear of one horse. That worked fine, until the other horse caught his ear on a barbed wire fence. Once again, the blonde couldn't tell them apart.

The neighbor then suggested that the blonde measure the horses for height. When she did, she was very pleased to find that the white horse was two inches taller than the black horse.

* * *

What do a blonde and an instant lottery ticket have in common?
All you have to do is scratch the box to win.

✳ ✳ ✳

A blonde is a bit overweight, so her doctor puts her on a diet.

"I want you to eat regularly for two days, then skip a day, and repeat the procedure for two weeks. The next time I see you, you'll have lost at least five pounds."

When the blonde returns, she's lost nearly twenty pounds.

"Why, that's amazing!" the doctor says. "Did you follow my instructions?"

The blonde nods. "I'll tell you what, though, I thought I was going to drop dead that third day."

"From hunger, you mean?" asked the doctor.

"No, from skipping," replied the blonde.

✳ ✳ ✳

What is the difference between a blonde and an inflatable doll?
About two cans of hair spray.

* * *

A blonde, a brunette, and a redhead went into a bar and ordered their drinks from the bartender.

Brunette: "I'll have a B and C."

Bartender: "What is a B and C?"

Brunette: "Bourbon and Coke."

Redhead: "And I'll have a G and T."

Bartender: "What's a G and T?"

Redhead: "Gin and tonic."

Blonde: "I'll have a 15."

Bartender: "What's a 15?"

Blonde: "7 and 7."

* * *

What's the quickest way to get into a blonde's pants?
Pick them up off the floor.

* * *

Blonde: "Excuse me, what time is it right now?"

Woman: "It's 11:25 p.m."

Blonde: (confused look on face) "You know, it's the weirdest thing. I've asked that question thirty times today, and every time someone gives me a different answer."

* * *

Where do blondes go to meet their relatives?
The vegetable garden.

* * *

A blonde kept trying to sell her old car, but didn't have any luck because the car had 340,000 miles on it. She discussed her problem with a brunette that she knew.

The brunette suggested, "There may be a chance to sell that car easier, but it's not going to be legal."

"That doesn't matter at all," replied the blonde. "All that matters is that I am able to sell this car."

"All right," replied the brunette. In a quiet voice, she told the blonde, "Here is the address of a friend of mine. He owns a car repair shop around here. Tell him I sent you, and he will turn the counter back on your car to 40,000 miles. Then it shouldn't be a problem to sell your car."

The following weekend, the blonde took a trip to the mechanic on the brunette's advice.

A month or so later, the brunette saw the blonde and asked, "Did you sell your car?"

"No!" replied the blonde. "Why should I? It only has 40,000 miles on it."

* * *

How many blondes does it take to play tag?
One.

* * *

On a deserted island there are three women: a blonde, a brunette, and a redhead. They needed to get back to the mainland but the only way is by swimming. The redhead goes first. She makes it a quarter of the way, then drowns. The brunette goes second. She makes it one-third of the way, then drowns. The blonde goes last. She makes it one-half of the way, gets tired, so turns back.

* * *

What is the connection between a blonde and a halogen headlamp?
They both get screwed on the front of a Ford Escort.

✳ ✳ ✳

A blonde and a brunette decide to start a farm together. They add up their life savings into a total of $200. The blonde then decides she wants to purchase a bull with the money. The brunette agrees, and so the blonde heads off to find the perfect bull. When she does, she is to send a telegram to the brunette and tell her to come get the bull.

Finally, the blonde finds the bull of her dreams. The farmer says he wants $200 for it. The blonde, thinking she can get a better deal, says no to his offer.

The farmer then says, "All right then, I'll give you a great deal, how about $199?"

The blonde accepts the offer and buys the bull. She has $1.00 left for the telegram. The telegram guy says, "It's $1.00 per word." The blonde thinks about this and says, "'Comfortable,' write that."

"Comfortable?" the guy questions.

"Yes," the blonde replies. "You see, she reads slow."

✳ ✳ ✳

There was a blonde who was so dumb that she . . . locked herself in a restroom and wet her pants.

* * *

Once there was a young blonde who really needed some money. She saw an ad in the newspaper for a job at an Elmo factory. She went down and applied, but the manager told her that she wouldn't want the job because it was so boring. The blonde begged him and said she would do anything because she needed the money really bad. After long consideration, the manager hired her.

A few hours later, the manager looked at the video monitor showing the factory floor and saw that the conveyer belt was backed up. The manager went downstairs to find out what the problem was. When he arrived, he saw that the blonde was sewing two marbles into the crotch of every Elmo.

The manager then told the blonde, "I said to give each Elmo two test tickles, not two testicles!"

* * *

A blonde stormed up to the front desk of the library and said, "I have a complaint!"

"Yes, Ma'am?" said the librarian, looking up at her.

"I borrowed a book last week and it was horrible!"

Puzzled by her complaint, the librarian asked, "What was wrong with it?"

"It had way too many characters and there was no plot whatsoever!" said the blonde.

The librarian nodded and said, "Ahhh. So you must be the person who took our phone book."

✳ ✳ ✳

A blonde once heard that milk baths would make you beautiful. She left a note for her milkman to leave 15 gallons of milk. When the milkman read the note, he felt there must be a mistake. He thought she probably meant 1.5 gallons, so he knocked on the door to clarify the order. The blonde came to the door, and the milkman said, "I found your note to leave 15 gallons of milk. Did you mean 15 gallons or 1.5 gallons?"

The blonde said, "I want 15 gallons. I'm going to fill my bathtub up with milk and take a milk bath."

The milkman then asked, "Oh, all right, would

you like it pasteurized?"

The blonde replied, "No, just up to my waist."

✳ ✳ ✳

How does a blonde make instant pudding?
She places the box in the microwave and looks for the "instant pudding" button.

✳ ✳ ✳

A young blonde is distraught because she fears her husband is having an affair, so she goes to a gun shop and buys a handgun. The next day, she comes home to find her husband in bed with a beautiful redhead. The blonde grabs the gun and holds it to her own head. The husband jumps out of bed, begging and pleading with her not to shoot herself. Hysterically, the blonde responds to the husband, "Shut up—you're next!"

✳ ✳ ✳

What do you call twenty-four blondes in a cardboard box?
A case of empties.

* * *

This blonde was at a vending machine. She put her change in, pressed a button, and out comes a drink. So she puts some more change in, pushes another button, and out comes another drink.

She keeps putting change in and pushing buttons and getting drinks. A man comes along and asks the blonde if she is going to be done at this machine any time soon, and she responds, "I'm not gonna quit until I stop winning."

* * *

A blonde goes for a job interview in an office. The interviewer decides to start with the basics. "So, Miss, can you tell us your age, please?"

The blonde counts carefully on her fingers for about thirty seconds before replying, "Uh . . . twenty-two!"

The interviewer tries another straightforward one to break the ice.

"And can you tell us your height, please?"

The young lady stands up and produces a measuring tape from her handbag. She then puts one end under her foot and extends the tape to the top of her head. She checks the measurement and announces, "Five foot two!"

This isn't looking good so the interviewer goes for the real basics.

"And, uh, just to confirm for our records—your name, please?"

The blonde bobs her head from side-to-side for about twenty seconds, mouthing something silently to herself, before replying "Mandy!"

The interviewer is completely baffled at this stage, so he asks, "Just out of curiosity, Miss, we can understand your counting on your fingers to work out your age, and the measuring tape for your height is obvious, but what were you doing when we asked you your name?"

"Oh, that!" replies the blonde. "That's just me running through 'Happy birthday to you, happy birthday to you . . . .'"

❋ ❋ ❋

What is the blonde's highest ambition in life?
She wants to be like Vanna White and learn the alphabet.

❋ ❋ ❋

Why did the blonde call the welfare office?
She wanted to know how to cook food stamps!

✳ ✳ ✳

A blonde went to a flight school, insisting she wanted to learn to fly.

As all the planes were currently in use, the owner agreed to instruct her by radio on how to pilot the solo helicopter.

He took her out, showed her how to start it and gave her the basics, and sent her on her way. After she climbed 1,000 feet, she radioed in. "I'm doing great! I love it! The view is so beautiful, and I'm starting to get the hang of this."

After 2,000 feet, she radioed again, saying how easy it was to fly. The instructor watched her climb over 3,000 feet, and was beginning to worry that she hadn't radioed in. A few minutes later, he watched in horror as she crashed about half a mile away. He ran over and pulled her from the wreckage. When he asked what happened, she said, "I don't know! Everything was going fine, but as I got higher, I was starting to get cold. I can barely remember anything after I turned off the big fan!"

* * *

What do you call a blonde with a dollar bill on her head?
All-you-can-eat-under-a-buck.

* * *

Three women are about to be executed for crimes. One's a brunette, one's a redhead, and one's a blonde. Two guards bring the brunette forward, and the executioner asks if she has any last requests. She says no, and the executioner shouts, "Ready . . . Aim . . ." Suddenly, the brunette yells "Earthquake!" Everyone is startled and looks around. She manages to escape.

The angry guards then bring the redhead forward, and the executioner asks if she has any last requests. She says no, and the executioner shouts, "Ready . . . Aim . . ." The redhead then screams, "Tornado!" Yet again, everyone is startled and looks around. She, too, escapes execution.

By this point, the blonde has figured out what the others did. The guards bring her forward, and the executioner asks if she has any last requests. She also says no, and the executioner shouts, "Ready . . . Aim . . ."

The blonde shouts, "Fire!"

＊ ＊ ＊

Why is a blonde like a hardware store?
They are both 10¢ a screw!

＊ ＊ ＊

What's the difference between a blonde and a solar-powered calculator?
The blonde works in the dark!

＊ ＊ ＊

A blond guy gets home early from work and hears strange noises coming from the bedroom. He rushes upstairs to find his wife naked on the bed, sweating and panting. "What's up?" he says. "I'm having a heart attack," cries the woman.

He rushes downstairs to grab the phone, but just as he's dialing, his four-year-old son comes up and says, "Daddy! Daddy! Uncle Ted's hiding in your closet and he's got no clothes on!" The guy slams the phone down and storms upstairs into the bedroom, past his screaming wife, and rips open the closet door.

Sure enough, there is his brother, totally naked, cowering on the floor.

"You rotten bastard," says the husband. "My wife's having a heart attack and you're running around naked, scaring the kids!"

✳ ✳ ✳

Why did the blonde tattoo her zip code on her stomach?
So her male would get delivered to the right box.

✳ ✳ ✳

An overweight blonde consulted her doctor for advice. The doctor advised that she run ten miles a day for thirty days. This, he promised, would help her lose as many as twenty pounds. The blonde followed the doctor's advice, and, after thirty days, she was pleased to find that she had indeed lost the pesky twenty pounds. She phoned the doctor and thanked him for the wonderful advice. At the end of the conversation, however, she asked the doc one last question: "How do I get home, since I am now 300 miles away?"

✳ ✳ ✳

Why did the blonde have tire-tread marks on her back?
From crawling across the street when the sign said: "Don't Walk."

* * *

The Blonde Nurse's Dictionary:
 Anally—occurring yearly
 Artery—study of paintings
 Bacteria—back door of cafeteria
 Barium—what doctors do when treatment fails
 Bowel—letter like A.E.I.O.U
 Caesarian section—district in Rome
 Cat scan—searching for kitty
 Cauterize—made eye contact with her
 Colic—sheep dog
 Coma—a punctuation mark
 Congenital—friendly
 D&C—where Washington is
 Diarrhea—journal of daily events
 Dilate—to live long
 Enema—not a friend
 Fester—quicker
 Fibula—a small lie
 Genital—non-Jewish
 Grippe—suitcase

Hangnail—coat hook

Impotent—distinguished, well-known

Intense pain—torture in a teepee

Labor pain—got hurt at work

Medical staff—doctor's cane

Morbid—higher offer

Nitrate—cheaper than day rate

Node—was aware of

Outpatient—person who had fainted

Pap smear—fatherhood test

Pelvis—cousin of Elvis

Post operative—letter carrier

Protein—favoring young people

Rectum—damn near killed 'em

Recovery room—place to do upholstery

Rheumatic—amorous

Scar—rolled tobacco leaf

Secretion—hiding anything

Seizure—Roman emperor

Serology—study of knighthood

Tablet—small table

Terminal illness—sickness at airport

Tibia—country in North Africa

Tumor—an extra pair

Urine—opposite of you're out

Varicose—located nearby

Vein—conceited

Brunette
Jokes

Why is a brunette like a bedspread?
They both get turned down every night.

* * *

Why did God give brunettes vaginas?
So men would talk to them.

* * *

Why does it take brunettes longer to have orgasms?
Who cares?

* * *

What's the difference between a brunette and a bowling ball?
You can only fit three fingers in a bowling ball.

* * *

What is a brunette's motto?
"Save a tree! Eat a beaver!"

* * *

What's the most common pick-up line brunettes hear?
How now, brown cow?

* * *

What do you get when you cross an elephant and a brunette?
A two-ton pickup.

* * *

How are brunettes like rocks?
You skip the flat ones.

* * *

Why can't Helen Keller drive?
She's a brunette.

* * *

How do you know a brunette is really fat?
She sits on your face and you can't hear the stereo.

* * *

How do you know a brunette is having her period?
She's only wearing one sock.

* * *

How do you get a brunette off your doorstep?
Pay for the pizza.

* * *

What do you call a brunette who broke up with her boyfriend?
Homeless.

* * *

What is "making love?"
Something a brunette does while a man is fucking her.

* * *

A man goes jogging one day and passes a hooker hanging around on the corner. "How much?"

he asks.

"Fifty bucks."

"How about ten?"

"Forget it."

So he goes on. The next morning, his brunette wife decides to join him on his jog. Soon they come to the hooker, staking out the same corner. "See what you get for ten bucks!" the hooker sneers.

✳ ✳ ✳

What do you do if a brunette and a lawyer are drowning and you can only save one of them?
Go to lunch and take home a movie.

✳ ✳ ✳

What's a brunette's favorite nursery rhyme?
Humpme Dumpme.

✳ ✳ ✳

Why do brunettes give great head?
They have to.

✳ ✳ ✳

What's the difference between a rabbi and a brunette?
A rabbi cuts it off. A brunette sucks it off.

* * *

A brunette and a blonde both jump off the Empire State Building at the same time. What happens to them?
The brunette goes splat. The blonde gets lost.

* * *

What do brunettes use for birth control?
Their personalities.

* * *

What's the ideal weight for a brunette?
About three pounds, including the urn.

* * *

How is a brunette like a toilet seat?
Without the hole in the middle, neither is worth a shit.

* * *

What's the difference between a brunette's clitoris and a golf ball?
A man will spend a half an hour looking for a golf ball.

* * *

What's the difference between sperm and mayonnaise?
Mayonnaise doesn't hit the back of a brunette's throat at 30 mph.

* * *

Why did the brunette cross the road?
Who cares? Why isn't she in the kitchen fixing dinner?

* * *

What's the difference between a brunette and a hockey player?
A hockey player takes a shower after three periods.

❋ ❋ ❋

What's the difference between a brunette and mom's apple pie?
You can eat mom's apple pie.

❋ ❋ ❋

Why do brunettes spend so much time at beauty parlors?
The estimates alone take three hours.

❋ ❋ ❋

Why do brunettes wear high heels?
So their knuckles won't drag on the ground.

❋ ❋ ❋

Why do brunettes wear tampons when skydiving?
So they don't whistle on the way down.

❋ ❋ ❋

Why are brunettes never lonely?
They have boyfriends up the ass.

* * *

Why do brunettes like long skirts?
They hide the no-pest strips.

* * *

How do you break a brunette's finger?
Punch her in the nose.

* * *

Why are there no brunette ballerinas?
When they do splits, they stick to the floor.

* * *

What happens when a brunette forgets to pay her
garbage bill?
They stop delivering.

* * *

How can you tell if a brunette is wearing
pantyhose?
Her ankles swell when she farts.

* * *

Why did the guy trade a brunette for an outhouse?
The hole was smaller and the smell was better.

* * *

What does a brunette get when she fucks a midget?
Twerpies.

* * *

What does a brunette get when she fucks a bird?
Chirpies.

* * *

What does a brunette get when she fucks with a pussy full of ice cream?
Slurpies.

* * *

Why do brunettes have legs?
So they don't leave tracks like snails.

* * *

What's the difference between a brunette and a
bucket of crap?
The bucket.

* * *

How can you tell the brunette in the cow pasture?
She's the one without a bell.

* * *

How do you know a brunette is really fat?
*When she sits around the house, she really sits
around the house.*

* * *

Why do brunettes give such good head?
They'll swallow anything.

* * *

How can you tell a brunette is really fat?
She sprays her lawn with vinegar and oil and grazes.

* * *

Did you hear about the new make-up kit for brunettes?
It comes in a three-gallon drum with an ice cream scoop.

* * *

Why do brunettes hate jokes about AIDS?
They always get it in the end.

* * *

Why do brunettes like big game hunters?
They dive headfirst into the bush.

* * *

Why do brunettes like head lice?
It makes a handy snack.

* * *

Why are brunettes like cow patties?
The older they are, the easier they are to pick up.

* * *

Why do brunettes have periods?
Because they deserve them.

* * *

How does a brunette know she's had a good time
on a date?
When she throws her panties against the wall,
they stick.

* * *

What does a brunette with a yeast infection do?
Scratch and sniff.

* * *

What's the difference between sex with a young brunette and an old brunette?
Poly-Grip.

＊ ＊ ＊

Why did the brunette get her car insurance canceled?
She was rear-ended too often.

＊ ＊ ＊

What do you call a brunette with a chipped tooth?
An organ grinder.

＊ ＊ ＊

What is a brunette's favorite Chinese food?
Cream of Sum Yung Gai.

＊ ＊ ＊

How does a brunette hold her liquor?
By the ears.

＊ ＊ ＊

Why did the brunette decide to keep her car?
She found out she could blow its horn.

* * *

How do you save a brunette from drowning?
Throw her an anchor.

* * *

What's the difference between pussy and rhubarb?
Brunettes won't eat rhubarb.

* * *

How do you know if a brunette is ticklish?
Give her a couple test tickles.

* * *

What's the difference between a brunette and
a PC?
When a brunette goes down on you, its foreplay.
When a computer goes down on you, you're
fucked.

* * *

How is a golf course like a brunette?
Both have a hole in the middle of the rough.

* * *

Why did the brunette turn down the job offer?
They wanted to pay her what she was worth, but she wouldn't work that cheap.

* * *

What's the difference between a brunette and a bowling ball?
You can't eat a bowling ball.

* * *

What do you get when you shove french fries into a brunette's pussy?
Fish and chips.

* * *

What do brunettes and footballs have in common?
Pigskin.

* * *

How did the brunette get busted?
*The cops found fifty pounds of crack under
her dress.*

* * *

Why do brunettes love beans?
Bubble baths.

* * *

What do you call a brunette who practices birth
control?
Humanitarian.

* * *

Then there was the brunette girl who was so ugly
her parents hired another girl to play her in the
home videos.

✳ ✳ ✳

What's a brunette's favorite deodorant?
RAID.

✳ ✳ ✳

What do a brunette and an elephant have
in common?
They both roll on their back for peanuts.

✳ ✳ ✳

Why do brunettes love hunters?
They go deep in the bush.
They shoot more than once.
They eat what they shoot.

✳ ✳ ✳

An ugly, fat brunette walks into a bar with a parrot
on her shoulder. "I'll fuck the first guy who can
guess the weight of my parrot," she announces
loudly.

"Five hundred pounds," calls out one smart ass.
"Folks, we have a winner!"

* * *

What's the difference between an elephant and
a brunette?
One hundred pounds and a flannel shirt.

* * *

Why did the homely brunette swallow a pin?
So she could feel a prick inside her.

* * *

Then there was the brunette who was so big she
had her own zip code.

* * *

Save the Whales!
Harpoon a Brunette.

* * *

What's the best thing about dating a homeless
brunette?
You can drop her off anywhere.

✳ ✳ ✳

What's white and found in a brunette's panties?
Clitty litter.

✳ ✳ ✳

Brunettes are like mopeds.
*Both are fun to ride until someone sees you
on one.*

✳ ✳ ✳

What has four wheels and flies?
A brunette in a wheelchair.

✳ ✳ ✳

What did the brunette say when her dog started
licking her face?
"Down, boy!"

✳ ✳ ✳

Then there was the husband who took his brunette wife with him everywhere.
He couldn't stand kissing her good-bye.

* * *

Why did the brunette douche with Crest?
She heard it reduces cavities.

* * *

How do you recondition a brunette?
Shove a ten-pound ham up her pussy and pull out the bone.

* * *

A man comes home from work and finds his brunette girlfriend sliding down the banister. "What are you doing?" he asks.

"Warming up your dinner."

* * *

Why are a brunette's cunt and asshole so close together?
So you can carry her around like a bowling ball.

∗ ∗ ∗

Why do brunettes like sleeveless dresses?
They love the feel of wind blowing through their hair.

∗ ∗ ∗

Why don't brunettes care how big your dick is?
All cocks taste alike.

∗ ∗ ∗

How can you tell a chic brunette?
She's wearing open-toed bowling shoes.

∗ ∗ ∗

Why do brunette children wear shoes?
To keep them from biting their nails.

∗ ∗ ∗

Then there was the brunette girl who was so fat she could only play "Seek."

＊ ＊ ＊

Why does it cost a brunette $35,000 to have a baby?
$5,000 in medical expenses, and $30,000 to get someone to sleep with her.

＊ ＊ ＊

Why are brunettes so gullible?
They'll swallow anything.

＊ ＊ ＊

Then there was the brunette who died in a pie-eating contest.
The cow sat on her head.

＊ ＊ ＊

How is "The NFL Today" like "The Miss Brunette" contest?
Both are pigskin previews.

※ ※ ※

What's a brunette sandwich?
One that's so full of baloney you can't swallow it.

※ ※ ※

Why are brunettes lousy detectives?
They blow every case.

※ ※ ※

Why did the brunette storm out of the fast food joint?
She found out "Big Mac" was a hamburger.

※ ※ ※

Why did the brunette commit suicide?
She heard marriages are made in heaven.

※ ※ ※

How do we know brunettes aren't made of sugar and spice?
They smell like tuna.

* * *

Why are brunettes immune to men?
They've been inoculated so many times.

* * *

How do you know which brunette gives the best
blow job?
Word of mouth.

* * *

What do you call a brunette that gives head?
A lap dog.

* * *

Why did a brunette take a vibrator to the beach?
She wanted to shake and bake.

* * *

How does a brunette recharge her love life?
She changes the batteries.

✳ ✳ ✳

How did the brunette lawyer shock the court?
She dropped her briefs.

✳ ✳ ✳

What's the worst part of anal sex with a brunette?
Her tapeworm bites your dick.

✳ ✳ ✳

Why do brunettes love sodomy?
Any ass can do it.

✳ ✳ ✳

Having sex with a brunette on the rag is a case of mind over matter.
If you don't mind, it don't matter.

✳ ✳ ✳

Then there was the brunette who went on the two-week LSD diet.
She took two hits and lost fourteen days.

* * *

Then there was the brunette who was so ugly,
she went to an orgy and everyone wanted to play
"Dress Poker" with her.

* * *

What do brunettes wear to weddings?
Formal bowling shirts.

* * *

What's the difference between garbage and a
brunette?
Garbage gets picked up once a week.

* * *

Why did God invent booze?
So brunettes could get laid, too.

* * *

Why did God create brunettes?
Sheep can't cook.

✳ ✳ ✳

Why do brunettes smell?
So blind people can hate them, too.

✳ ✳ ✳

Why are brunettes so religious?
They like being passed around like collection plates.

✳ ✳ ✳

Why don't brunettes swim in the ocean?
They leave a ring.

✳ ✳ ✳

What's a brunette's idea of mixed luggage?
Two shopping bags from the same store.

✳ ✳ ✳

What do you call a brunette hitchhiker?
Stranded.

✳ ✳ ✳

Why does Ohio have brunettes and California have earthquakes?
California had first choice.

✳ ✳ ✳

Why don't brunettes have freckles?
They slide off.

✳ ✳ ✳

How do brunettes spell relief?
F-A-R-T.

✳ ✳ ✳

What do you call 288 brunettes?
Too gross.

✳ ✳ ✳

What football position are brunettes best at?
Wide receiver.

✳ ✳ ✳

What is brunettes' worst football position?
Tight end.

✳ ✳ ✳

A cannibal goes to a new cannibal restaurant, sits down, and looks over the menu. He notices blondes are $6.95, redheads are $7.95, and brunettes are $29.95. He calls the waiter over and asks, "How come brunettes are so expensive?"

"Have you ever tried cleaning one?"

✳ ✳ ✳

Why are blonde jokes so short?
So brunettes can remember them.

✳ ✳ ✳

What did the brunette say when she stepped in dog poop?
"Oh, no! I'm melting!"

✳ ✳ ✳

How do brunettes get rid of cockroaches?
They ask for commitment.

* * *

How does a pregnant brunette know her kid will grow up to be a lawyer?
She has a craving for bologna.

* * *

What's the difference between broccoli and boogers?
Brunettes won't eat broccoli.

* * *

How do brunettes make God laugh?
They tell him their plans for life.

* * *

What do you call the place a brunette sticks her gum on the way down?
Bellybutton.

✳ ✳ ✳

How long does a brunette cook her meat?
Until the tire marks go away.

✳ ✳ ✳

Then there was the brunette who was so big they baptized her at Sea World.

✳ ✳ ✳

What do old brunettes have between their tits that young brunettes don't?
Their bellybuttons.

✳ ✳ ✳

What do you get when you trade your brunette for a skunk?
A better-smelling pussy.

✳ ✳ ✳

What do you call Branson, Missouri?
Las Vegas for brunettes.

* * *

What do brunettes and drug dealers have in common?
Three-hundred pounds of crack.

* * *

How many brunettes does it take to stop a runaway bus?
Not enough.

* * *

What's the difference between a brunette and the tide?
A tide gets taken out.

* * *

What do you get when a blonde, a brunette, and a redhead get together?
Ménage-à-twat.

* * *

A man's wife, a typical brunette, got sick, so he took her to the doctor.

"I don't like the look of your wife," commented the doctor.

"Neither do I," replied the man, "but she's good with the kids."

✳ ✳ ✳

A brunette was vacationing in Miami, sunning herself on the beach. A handsome man came and settled in on the beach a few feet away.

"Hey, handsome, tell me about yourself," cooed the brunette.

"Well," replied the guy, "I just got finished serving three years for armed robbery, assault, and sexual battery."

"So you're single?"

✳ ✳ ✳

What's the difference between Hillary Clinton and a brunette?
Hillary only gives snow jobs.

✳ ✳ ✳

What's the toughest part of making love to
a brunette?
Setting up the "On" ramps.

* * *

Why do brunettes only make love from the bottom?
They only know how to fuck up.

* * *

What's the difference between a brunette and
a pizza?
There's less cheese on a pizza.

* * *

Why don't brunettes go to their daughters'
weddings?
Someone has to watch the baby.

* * *

What did the brunette say when she lost her
virginity?
"Thanks, Daddy!"

✳ ✳ ✳

Why are hangovers better than brunettes?
Hangovers go away.

✳ ✳ ✳

Why do men lie to brunettes?
They keep asking questions.

✳ ✳ ✳

A man goes to see his doctor and gets some bad news.

"I'm sorry," says the doc, "but you only have six months to live."

"Oh, my god! What am I going to do?" cries the man.

"Marry a brunette. It will be the longest six months of your life."

✳ ✳ ✳

How do you know when a brunette isn't wearing panties?
She has dandruff on her shoes.

* * *

What's the difference between a brunette and a bowling ball?
Your fingers don't smell after you stick them in a bowling bowl.

* * *

Why are brunettes so strong?
They have to support themselves.

* * *

Why did the brunette run away from home?
She didn't like the way her daddy was rearing her.

* * *

A brunette said to her boyfriend, "Let's play hide-and-seek. If you find me, I'll give you a blowjob."
   "But what if I can't find you?"
   "I'll be behind the couch."

* * *

What do brunettes usually call the first guy they screw?
"Brother."

* * *

Why do brunettes wear turtlenecks?
To hide the flea collars.

* * *

What do you call a 250-pound brunette?
Anorexic.

* * *

Why don't brunette girls get an allowance for being good?
Brunettes are good-for-nothing.

* * *

What's the difference between the wind and a brunette?
Some days the wind doesn't blow.

* * *

How do you know a brunette has moved in next door?
The cockroaches start eating out.

* * *

Why did the brunette stop using her dildo?
Telephone poles give splinters.

* * *

How do you get a brunette pregnant?
Come on her shoes and let the flies do the rest.

* * *

What does a brunette miss most about a party?
The invitation.

* * *

What is a brunette's mating call?
"Has that blonde bitch left yet?"

✳ ✳ ✳

How do you know a brunette has just lost her virginity?
Her crayons are sticky.

✳ ✳ ✳

What's the difference between a brunette and an ironing board?
The legs of an ironing board are hard to open.

✳ ✳ ✳

What's the difference between a brunette and a brick?
A brick doesn't follow you around, whining for a week after you lay it.

✳ ✳ ✳

How did the brunette burn her nose?
Bobbing for fries.

✳ ✳ ✳

Why did the brunette take a job at the loading dock?
She loved taking deliveries in the rear.

* * *

Why do brunettes use feminine deodorant spray?
For around-the-cock protection.

* * *

Why do brunettes have a speed limit of 68?
When they hit 69 they blow a rod.

* * *

What's the difference between Bigfoot and a brunette?
One is six feet tall, has matted hair, and stinks. The other just has big feet.

* * *

A blonde and brunette are walking down the street.
   "I smell cock," says the blonde.
   "Oh, that's just my breath," replies the brunette.

* * *

Why do brunettes like corduroys?
So they can whiffle while they work.

* * *

What do you call a brunette with a million dollars?
A cash cow.

* * *

What did the brunette do when she couldn't find her glasses?
She drank straight from the bottle.

* * *

Why do brunettes fake orgasm?
They think men care.

* * *

How do brunettes remove their make-up?
Easy Off.

* * *

Why did the brunette visit the pet cemetery?
To visit her childhood sweetheart.

* * *

What does a brunette put behind her ears to attract men?
Her knees.

* * *

Why did the brunette marry her dog?
She had to.

* * *

What's the difference between a whale and a brunette?
People like to "Save the Whales."

* * *

Then there was the honest brunette secretary.
She called in "lazy."

✳ ✳ ✳

Why do brunettes hate priests and Christmas trees?
The balls are just for decoration.

✳ ✳ ✳

What do you call three brunettes sitting on the lawn?
Fertilizer.

✳ ✳ ✳

A trucker stops at a little restaurant for the first time. The waitress, a brunette, comes over and says, "What would you like, Sugar?"

"I'd like a little pussy, he says, leering.

"So would I," the waitress replies. "Mine's huge."

✳ ✳ ✳

Why was the brunette late for her own wedding?
She couldn't find a clean bowling shirt.

✳ ✳ ✳

How does a brunette stop a dog from humping
her leg?
She gives him a blow job.

* * *

What did the brunette like most about sex
education?
Oral exams.

* * *

Why don't brunettes take showers?
Oil and water don't mix.

* * *

How does a brunette keep her youth?
She gives him lots of money.

* * *

Why did the brunette have twelve pairs of
underwear?
One for each month.

* * *

What's the worst advice you can give a brunette?
Be yourself.

* * *

Why was the brunette bisexual?
It doubled her chances for a date on Saturday night.

* * *

What's the difference between an elephant and a brunette?
The moustache and house dress.

* * *

What's a brunette's favorite drink?
A penis colada.

* * *

What's a brunette's worst dilemma?
A guy with a twelve-inch dick and herpes.

∗ ∗ ∗

What do brunettes do after sex?
Walk home.

∗ ∗ ∗

Why did the brunette take up jogging?
She wanted to hear heavy breathing.

∗ ∗ ∗

Then there was the brunette who treated her
husband like a god.
Every meal was a burnt offering.

∗ ∗ ∗

Why are brunettes the only women who
keep diaries?
Blondes and redheads don't have the time.

∗ ∗ ∗

Then there was the brunette who got her good looks from her father.
He was a plastic surgeon.

* * *

How are the Unibomber and a brunette alike?
They were both fingered by their brother.

* * *

Then there was the brunette who was so fat her insurance company offered her a group rate.

* * *

What's the difference between a brunette and a toothbrush?
You don't let your friends use your toothbrush.

* * *

What's the difference between a monkey and a brunette?
The monkey has fewer fleas.

✳ ✳ ✳

What do they throw at a brunette's wedding?
Puffed rice.

✳ ✳ ✳

How do you hide money from a brunette?
Put it in the bathtub.

✳ ✳ ✳

Then there was the brunette who had a wooden baby.
She got nailed by a carpenter.

✳ ✳ ✳

Streaking was invented by a brunette.
She confused Preparation H and Bengay.

✳ ✳ ✳

Then there was the brunette who thought diarrhea was hereditary.
She found it in her jeans.

* * *

Who won the brunette beauty contest?
Nobody.

* * *

Why do brunettes have pretty noses?
They're hand-picked.

* * *

Brunette: "I really hate my job."
    Blonde: "What do you do?"
    Brunette: "I clean-up after the elephants at
          the circus."
    Blonde: "Well, why don't you quit?"
    Brunette: "What? And give up show business?"

* * *

Why don't brunettes play hide-and-seek?
No one will look for them.

* * *

How do you break a brunette's finger?
Smack her in the nose.

* * *

What does a brunette say when she picks
her nose?
Grace.

* * *

Why do they bury brunettes with their butts sticking
out of the ground?
They make great bicycle racks.

* * *

Why were wheelbarrows invented?
To teach brunettes to walk on two legs.

* * *

How many brunettes does it take to make
chocolate-chip cookies?
*Two. One to make the dough and one to squeeze
the rabbit.*

* * *

What do you call a brunette behind a steering wheel?
An airbag.

* * *

What's the difference between a brunette and a 747?
Not everyone has been in a 747.

* * *

What's the difference between a beautiful brunette and Bigfoot?
Bigfoot's been spotted.

* * *

Why do little brunette girls put fish in their underwear?
So they can smell like big brunette girls.

* * *

What's a brunette "10"?
A brunette that fucks and sucks until midnight, then turns into a pizza and a six-pack.

* * *

Then there was the horny brunette bride that carried a bouquet of batteries.

* * *

Did you hear about the brunette who had two chances to get pregnant?
She blew both of them.

* * *

What's the difference between a dead brunette lying on the highway and a dead blonde lying on the highway?
There are skid marks in front of the blonde.

* * *

A brunette was making love to her boyfriend.

"Honey," she asked, "could you take your ring off? It's hurting me!"

"That's not my ring. That's my wristwatch!"

✳ ✳ ✳

What did the brunette give her South African boyfriend?
Apart-head.

✳ ✳ ✳

Why don't brunettes drink beer on the beach?
They're afraid of getting sand in their Schlitz.

✳ ✳ ✳

Why was the brunette thrown off of the beach?
The lifeguard caught her going down for the third time.

✳ ✳ ✳

What do you call ripping off a brunette's
pantyhose?
Foreplay.

* * *

A brunette's three biggest lies:
1. You're the biggest.
2. You're the best.
3. It doesn't always smell this way.

* * *

What chain of stores do brunettes patronize?
Stop 'N' Blow.

* * *

What is a brunette's favorite rock group?
Yes.

* * *

What do you call a brunette who uses the
rhythm method?
Mom.

✳ ✳ ✳

What does a brunette wear to a funeral?
A black bowling shirt.

✳ ✳ ✳

What would be great about electing a brunette president?
We wouldn't have to pay her as much.

✳ ✳ ✳

Then there was the brunette mutant with tits on her back.
She was funny to look at, but fun to dance with.

✳ ✳ ✳

What's the difference between a brunette fox and a brunette pig?
Eight beers.

✳ ✳ ✳

Why do brunettes chew with their mouths closed?
Keeps out the flies.

* * *

What's the difference between a brunette and
a redhead?
Brunettes crunch when you eat them.

* * *

What's twenty-feet long with a rancid smell?
Ten brunettes line-dancing.

* * *

A brunette went to visit a psychiatrist.
  "Doctor, everybody hates me!" she complained.
  "Don't be silly," replied the shrink. "Not
everybody has met you."

* * *

What do a brunette and a Yeti have in common?
They are both abominable.

✳ ✳ ✳

Then there was the brunette whose dress fit her like a glove.
It stuck out in five places.

✳ ✳ ✳

Then there was the brunette that put Odor Eaters in her shoes.
She disappeared.

✳ ✳ ✳

Then there was the ugly brunette lesbian.
She had to go out with guys.

✳ ✳ ✳

How do you sit four brunettes in a crowded bar?
Turn a stool upside-down.

✳ ✳ ✳

What is a brunette's favorite bread?
Humpernickel.

* * *

What do you give a brunette for Christmas?
Gift-wrapped batteries.

* * *

What's the difference between a light bulb and
a brunette?
You can unscrew a light bulb.

* * *

There was a brunette standing alongside a busy
road chanting "88, 88, 88, 88 . . ."

A blonde came up to her and said, "That looks
like fun, can I try?"

The brunette said, "Sure."

So the blonde chanted, "88, 88, 88, 88 . . ."

"Well," said the brunette, "that is fun. But what
is even more fun is if you say it in the middle of
the street."

So the blonde said, "OK" and stood in the

middle of the street saying "88, 88, 88, 88-" and BAM! She was run-over by a car, completely flattened.

Along the side of the road, the brunette began to chant, "89, 89, 89, 89 . . . ."

✳ ✳ ✳

There were eleven people holding onto a rope that came down from a plane. Ten were blonde, and one was a brunette. They all decided that one person should get off because if they didn't, then the rope would break and everyone would die. No one could decide who should go, so finally the brunette said, "I'll get off." After a really touching speech from the brunette saying she would get off, all of the blondes started clapping.

✳ ✳ ✳

Why did they call the brunette "Twinkie"?
She liked to be filled with cream.

✳ ✳ ✳

Did you hear the one about the brunette who thought that "love handles" referred to her ears?

* * *

What's the difference between a brunette and a telephone?
It costs fifty cents to use a telephone.

* * *

What's the difference between a brunette and a computer?
You only have to punch information into a computer once.

* * *

What do you get when you cross a brunette and a gorilla?
Who knows, there is only so much a gorilla can be forced to do.

* * *

Why did God create brunettes?
Because sheep can't bring beer from the fridge.

* * *

What is the difference between a brunette and
a mosquito?
The mosquito stops sucking after you smack it.

* * *

A blonde, a brunette, a movie star, the pope, and a
pilot were on a plane.

The plane was going down fast, and there were
only four parachutes for all five of them. The pilot
took one and jumped, then the movie star took
one and jumped, and then the blonde took one
and jumped. The pope told the brunette to take
the last one. The brunette said, "There are still two
parachutes left! The blonde took my backpack!"

* * *

What's on a brunette's TV?
Dust.

* * *

A fellow picked up a brunette in a bar and took her home with him. After some preliminary drinks and talk, they got undressed and climbed into bed. After a few minutes, the brunette started laughing. The fellow asked her what she found so amusing.

"Your organ," she replied. "It's a bit on the small side."

Hurt, he replied, "It's not used to playing in cathedrals."

✳ ✳ ✳

A brunette had been married about a year.

One day, she came running up to her husband, jumping for joy.

He didn't know how to react, so he started jumping up and down along with her.

"Why are we so happy?" he asked.

She said, "Honey, I have some really great news for you!"

"Great," he said. "Tell me what you're so happy about."

She stopped, breathless from all the jumping.

"I'm pregnant!" she gasped.

The husband was ecstatic, as they had been trying for quite a while.

He grabbed her, and kissed her.

"Wow, that is wonderful! I couldn't be happier."

Then she said, "Oh, honey, there's more."

"What do you mean 'more'?" he asked.

"Well, we are not having just one baby, we are going to have TWINS!"

He was amazed at how she could know so soon after getting pregnant.

"How do you know that?" he asked.

"It was easy," she said. "I went to the pharmacy and bought the two-pack home pregnancy test. Both tests came out positive!"

✳ ✳ ✳

What's the real reason a brunette keeps her figure? *No one else wants it.*

✳ ✳ ✳

A brunette fell for her handsome new dentist like a ton of bricks and pretty soon had lured him into a series of passionate rendezvous in the dental clinic after hours.

But one day he said sadly, "Honey, we have to stop seeing each other. Your husband's bound to get suspicious."

"No way, sweetie, he's dumb as a post," she

assured him. "Besides, we've been meeting here for six months now and he doesn't suspect a thing."

"True," agreed the dentist, "but you're down to one tooth!"

* * *

Why are brunettes so proud of their hair?
It matches their mustache.

* * *

A young man took a brunette out to dinner and a show. They got along very well, and when he asked her if she would like to come up to his apartment for a drink, she agreed. After they were at the apartment awhile, they began to make love, and he asked if he could give her an old-fashioned kiss.

"Gee," says the brunette, "at a time like this you want me to change positions?"

* * *

A guy takes a brunette out on her first date. When they pull-off into a secluded area around midnight, the brunette says, "My mother told me to say 'no' to everything."

"Well," the guy says, "do you mind if I put my arm around you?"

"No," the girl replied.

"Do you mind if I put my other hand on your leg?"

"N-n-no," the girl replied.

"You know," says the guy, "keep saying 'no' and we're going to have a whole lotta fun tonight!"

* * *

Why are most brunettes flat-chested?
It makes it easier to read their T-shirts.

* * *

Why do brunettes like their dark hair color?
It doesn't show the dirt.

* * *

A huge guy marries a tiny brunette and at the wedding, one of his friends says to him, "How the hell do the two of you have sex?"

The big guy says, "I just sit there, naked on a chair, while she sits on top and I bob her up-

and-down."

His friend says, "You know, that don't sound too bad."

The big guy says, "Well, it's kind of like jerking off, only I got somebody to talk to."

✳ ✳ ✳

A brunette gets a tattoo of Santa Claus on one thigh and a turkey on the other. She wants to show that there is something good to eat between Thanksgiving and Christmas.

✳ ✳ ✳

Why didn't Indians scalp brunettes?
The hair from a buffalo's butt was more manageable.

✳ ✳ ✳

A redhead from Texas and a brunette from New York were seated side-by-side on an airplane. The redhead from Texas, being friendly and all, said: "So, where y'all from?"

The New York brunette said, "From a place

where they know better than to use a preposition at the end of a sentence."

The redhead from Texas sat quietly for a few moments and then replied, "So, where y'all from, bitch?"

✳ ✳ ✳

Who makes bras for brunettes?
Fisher-Price.

✳ ✳ ✳

How can you tell if a brunette is lonely?
Check her for a pulse.

✳ ✳ ✳

Why do brunettes wear training bras?
Because it's cheaper than changing their band-aids everyday.

✳ ✳ ✳

Why does it take five brunettes to change a
light bulb?
To help out the blonde that's been trying for weeks.

✳ ✳ ✳

Why was the first football stadium sketched out on
a brunette's chest?
Because they needed a level playing field.

✳ ✳ ✳

Why do brunettes put ice in their nose before they
go to work?
So their lunch won't spoil.

✳ ✳ ✳

Why can't brunettes "tease" their hair?
Because it's not funny.

✳ ✳ ✳

What do you call going on a blind date with
a brunette?
Brown-bagging it.

✳ ✳ ✳

A nurse at the hospital received a call from an anxious patient.

"I'm diabetic and I'm afraid I've had too much sugar today," the caller said.

"Are you light-headed?" the nurse asked.

"No," the caller answered, "I'm a brunette."

✳ ✳ ✳

What do you call a brunette who gets a call on Saturday night?
Startled.

✳ ✳ ✳

Why do blondes always hang out with brunettes?
Because it makes the blondes look smart.

✳ ✳ ✳

Why did God create brunettes?
So ugly guys would have someone to date.

✳ ✳ ✳

A brunette and her husband were invited to a
swanky masked Halloween Party. At the last minute,
the brunette got a terrible headache and told
her husband to go to the party alone. He, being
a devoted husband, protested, but the brunette
argued and said she was going to take some
aspirin and go to bed, and there was no need for
him to miss the party. So he took his costume and
away he went.

The wife, after sleeping soundly for one hour,
awakened without pain, and as it was still early, she
decided to go to the party, too. Her husband did not
know what her costume was, so she thought she
would have some fun by watching him to see how
he acted when she was not with him.

The brunette joined the party and soon spotted
her husband cavorting around on the dance
floor, dancing with every nice chick he could, and
copping a little feel here, and a little kiss there. His
wife sidled-up to him and began to flirt with him.

As she was dancing with him, she let him go
as far as he wished (naturally, since he was her
husband). Finally, he whispered a little proposition
in her ear and she agreed, so off they went to
one of the cars and had a little bang. Just before
unmasking at midnight, she slipped away and went
home. She put her costume away and got into bed,
wondering what kind of excuse her husband would

make for his behavior.

She was reading when he came in. She asked him how his night had gone and he replied, "Oh, it was the same old thing. You know I never have a good time when you're not there." Then she asked, "Did you dance much?"

He replied, "I never even danced once. When I got there, I met Pete, Bill, Ted, and some other guys, so we went into the den and played poker all evening. But get this, the guy I loaned my costume to sure had a real good time!"

✳ ✳ ✳

Why are there no dumb brunette jokes?
Because blondes would have to think them up.

✳ ✳ ✳

A brunette's husband had been slipping in and out of a coma for several months, yet she had stayed by his bedside every single day. One day, when he came to, he motioned for her to come nearer. As she sat by him, he whispered, eyes full of tears, "You know what? You have been with me all through the bad times. When I got fired, you were there to support me. When my business failed, you were there. When I got shot, you were by my side. When we lost the house, you stayed right here. When my health started failing, you were still by my side. You know what?"

"What, dear?" the brunette asked gently, smiling as her heart began to fill with warmth.

"I think you're bad luck."

✳ ✳ ✳

What's so good about brunette midgets?
They're only half as ugly.

✳ ✳ ✳

A brunette gets on a bus with her baby. The bus driver says: "That's the ugliest baby that I've ever seen. Ugh!"

The woman goes to the rear of the bus and sits down, fuming. She says to a man next to her: "The driver just insulted me!"

The man says: "You go right up there and tell him off—go ahead, I'll hold your monkey for you."

✳ ✳ ✳

Why are brunettes like tires?
There's always a spare.

* * *

Why do brunettes have arms?
Have you any idea how long it would take to lick a bathroom clean?

* * *

How do you piss-off a brunette during sex?
Call her on the phone.

* * *

What do you call an open can of tuna in a brunette's apartment?
Potpourri.

* * *

A rather heavy brunette showed up at the theatre just before the performance started and handed the usher two tickets.

"Where's the other party?" asked the usher.

"Well," said the lady, with a blush, "you see, one seat is a little small for me and rather uncomfortable, so I bought two. But they're both really for me."

"Okay with me, lady," the usher replied, scratching his head. "There's just one problem. Your seats are numbers fifty-one and sixty-three."

* * *

How can you tell a sumo wrestler from a brunette?
A Sumo wrestler shaves his legs.

* * *

A brunette was shaking out a rug on the balcony of her 17th-floor condominium when a sudden gust of wind blew her over the railing.

"Damn, that was stupid," she thought as she fell. "What a way to die."

As the brunette passed the 14th floor, a man standing at his railing caught her in his arms. While she looked at him with unbelievable gratitude, he asked, "Do you swallow?"

"No!" she shrieked, aghast.

So, he dropped her. As she passed the 12th floor, another man reached out and caught her.

"Do you screw?" he asked.

"Of course not!" she exclaimed before she could stop herself. He dropped her, too.

The poor brunette prayed to God for one more chance. As luck would have it, she was caught a third time, by a man on the 8th floor.

"I swallow! I screw!" she screamed in panic.

"Slut!" he said, and dropped her.

❋ ❋ ❋

Why do brunettes have more brains than cows?
So when you pull their tits they won't shit on the floor.

❋ ❋ ❋

What do horny brunettes order at Subway?
Footlongs.

❋ ❋ ❋

A little brunette girl was playing in a tree near a church. The priest was taking a walk when he happened to look up the tree and saw the little girl. She had no panties on. He called her down and gave her money to buy a pair of panties. The girl was so happy, she ran home and told her brunette mommy about it. The next day when the priest was again taking his daily walk, he looked up the same tree and saw the young girl's mother up there. She had no panties on. He called her down and gave her two dollars to go buy a razor.

✳ ✳ ✳

Two fat brunettes are in a dyke bar.

One says to the other, "Your round."

The other one says, "So are you, you fat pig!"

✳ ✳ ✳

What's the difference between Bigfoot and a brunette?

A brunette is better in bed.

✳ ✳ ✳

How do you teach a brunette math?

Subtract her clothes, divide her legs, and square root her.

✳ ✳ ✳

Getting married to a brunette is very much like going to a restaurant with friends. You order what you want, then when you see what the other fellow has, you wish you had ordered that.

＊ ＊ ＊

A guy was dating a religious brunette. She was a moral woman who had remained a virgin despite his efforts to seduce her. In fact, he had never even seen her naked and it was driving him crazy.

One day, the brunette remarked about how slowly he drove.

"I can't stand it anymore," she told him. "Let's play a game. For every five miles per hour over the speed limit you drive, I'll remove one piece of clothing."

He enthusiastically agreed and sped up the car.

He reached the 55 mph mark, so she took off her blouse.

At 60, off came her pants.

At 65, it was her bra, and at 70, her panties.

Now, seeing her naked for the first time and traveling faster than he ever had before, he became very excited and lost control of the car. He veered off the road, went over an embankment, and hit a tree. The brunette was not hurt, but he was trapped.

She tried to pull him free, but alas he was stuck.

"Go to the road and get help," he said. "I don't have anything to cover myself with!" she replied. The man felt around, but could only reach one of his shoes. "You'll have to put this between your legs to cover up," he told her.

So the brunette did as he said and went up to the road for help. Along came a truck driver. Seeing a naked, crying young woman along the road, he pulled over to hear her story.

"My boyfriend! My boyfriend!" she sobbed. "He's stuck and I can't pull him out!"

The truck driver looked down at the shoe between her legs and replied, "Ma'am, if he's in that far, I'm afraid he's a goner!"

✳ ✳ ✳

Then there was the brunette who was soooooooo fat, she . . .

had to wake up in sections.

stepped on a scale and it said, "To be continued."

had her baby pictures taken by satellite.

had a bellybutton that made an echo.

played hopscotch like, "Texas...Alabama...North Carolina...Pennsylvania..."

had a cereal bowl that came with a lifeguard.
left footprints in hard concrete!
said, "Trick or Meatloaf!" on Halloween.
had so many double chins she looked like she
    was staring over a pile of pancakes.
stepped on a scale and it said, "No livestock,
    please."
her friends took a train and two busses just to
    get to her good side.
had people jog around her for exercise.
jumped into the Gulf in Panama City and the
    tide came in at Myrtle Beach.
had her own area code.
had NASA orbiting satellites around her.
showed up on radar.
used her belt to measure the earth's equator.
had Goodyear trying to fly her over the
    Super Bowl.

✳ ✳ ✳

A profoundly ugly brunette went to the psychiatrist.

"My life is a mess, doctor," she began, "I am so hideous that no one will associate with me, touch me, or even talk to me. Can you help?"

"Why, certainly!" the psychiatrist said. "Helping people feel much better about themselves is my area of expertise. I can start making you feel more confident about your appearance right here and now."

"Oh, I am so grateful! What should I do first?" she asked.

"First things first. Just walk over to the other side of the room and lie face-down on my couch."

❋ ❋ ❋

A brunette sat sobbing in the police station. "I was raped by an Italian," she wailed.

"How do you know he was an Italian?" the detective asked.

"I had to help him," the brunette replied.

❋ ❋ ❋

What's the difference between a brunette and a bathtub?
You can scrub the scum off a bathtub.

❋ ❋ ❋

A brunette walked into an orchard and found a lovely pond, so she decided to go for a swim. She looked around, didn't see anyone, and undressed. Just as she was about to dive in, the watchman appeared from behind the bush where he was hiding all along and told her that swimming was prohibited.

"You could have told me that before I undressed!" she scolded him.

"Hey! Only swimming is prohibited, undressing isn't," he replied.

✳ ✳ ✳

A brunette goes to the doctor. She says, "Doc, I'm freaking' out! My pee's coming out in four streams."

He says, "Get up on the table and I'll see what I can do."

She gets up on the table, and as he's examining her, he starts to giggle.

She says, "It's not funny. My pee's coming out in four streams."

He says, "It won't anymore. I took the trouser button out of there."

✳ ✳ ✳

What's the difference between your job and a dead brunette?
Your job still sucks.

* * *

A guy meets a brunette out at a nightclub and she invites him back to her place for the night. They get back to her house and they go into her bedroom. The guy notices all these fluffy toys, hundreds of them—fluffy toys on top of the wardrobe, fluffy toys on the bookshelf and window sill on the floor, and of course, fluffy toys all over the bed. Later, after they've had sex, he turns to her and asks, "So, how was I?"

She says, "Well . . . you can take anything from the bottom shelf."

* * *

An old man of 90 married a young brunette of 18. When they got into bed the night after the wedding, he held up three fingers.

"Oh, honey," said the young brunette. "Does that mean we're going to do it three times?"

"No," said the old man. "It means you can take your pick."

* * *

One brunette could have had any man she pleased.
She just couldn't please any.

* * *

Brunettes have feelings, too.
But who cares?

* * *

How does a brunette know dinner is ready?
The smoke alarm goes off.

* * *

Being brunette is one of those bad things that
happen to good people.

* * *

A pretty brunette loved growing tomatoes, but
couldn't seem to get her tomatoes to turn red.
One day, while taking a stroll , she came upon a
gentleman neighbor who had the most beautiful

garden full of huge red tomatoes. The brunette asked the gentleman, "What do you do to get your tomatoes so red?"

The gentleman responded, "Well, twice a day I stand in front of my tomato garden and expose myself and my tomatoes turn red from blushing so much."

Well, the woman was so impressed, she decided to try doing the same thing to her tomato garden to see if it would work. So twice a day for two weeks, she exposed herself to her garden hoping for the best.

One day, the gentleman was passing by and asked the brunette, "By the way, how did you make out? Did your tomatoes turn red?"

"No," she replied, "but my cucumbers are enormous."

✳ ✳ ✳

Brunettes are like fast food.
Quick, cheap and easy.

✳ ✳ ✳

The brunette knelt in the confessional and said, "Bless me, Father, for I have sinned."

"What is it, child?"

"Father, I have committed the sin of vanity. Twice a day I gaze at myself in the mirror and tell myself how beautiful I am."

The priest turned, took a good look at the girl, and said, "My dear, I have good news. That isn't a sin . . . it's simply a mistake."

∗ ∗ ∗

A young brunette girl of fourteen went to work in a broom factory. After two months, she gave the boss a two-week notice. The boss was quite unhappy to let her go since she was so hard-working. He called her into his office to find out the reason. "But why?" he asked.

"It's nothing, I just wanna quit, that's all," she said, sullenly.

"Look, I'll give you a raise."

"No," she said.

"You can't just quit like that. There must be a reason. Tell me."

"OK, if you must know . . ." said the girl, and she took off her underwear and pointed to her pubic hair. "Look! I haven't had this before—it's the broom's bristles, I tell you."

Tickled by her innocence, he took off his

underwear and showed it to her, saying, Ha ha! My dear, it's nature. Look . . . I have it, too!"

"Oh, no!" the girl cried. "I can't wait two weeks, I quit now! Not only do you have the bristles, but you've grown the handle as well."

* * *

How can you tell if a brunette is dead?
The sex is the same but the dishes pile up.

* * *

One day, a little girl was sitting and watching her mother do the dishes at the kitchen sink. She suddenly noticed that her mother had several strands of white hair sticking out from her panties in contrast to her brunette hair. She looked at her mother and asked inquisitively, "Why are some of your hairs white, Mom?

Her mother replied, "Well, every time that you do something wrong and make me cry or unhappy, one of my hairs turns white.

The little girl thought about this revelation for a while and then asked, "Mama, how come ALL of grandma's hairs are white?"

* * *

A brunette sees three dogs in the park and kneels down to pet them. "What's your name?" she asks the first dog. To her surprise, the dog answers. "My name's Huey and I'm having a great day going in and out of puddles." She goes up to the second dog and asks, "What's your name?" The dog replies, "My name's Duey and I'm having a great day going in and out of puddles." She turns to the third dog and says, "I suppose you're going to tell me your name's Luey and you're having a great day going in and out of puddles, too." The dog replies, "No, I'm having a fucking miserable day and my name is Puddles."

* * *

The brunette had a very sympathetic face.
It has everyone's sympathy.

* * *

Then there was the brunette who had so many wrinkles, she had to screw her hat on.

* * *

Brunettes take vitamins A, B, C, D, E, F, and G, and still looks like H.

* * *

Don't forget the brunette who drinks so much she's been nominated for the "Alcohol of Fame."

* * *

The brunette bride was so fat, when she walked down the aisle with her groom, they had to go single file.

* * *

A brunette saved for years to buy an unbreakable, waterproof, shockproof watch—and then she lost it.

* * *

Brunettes love going to the movies.
They get to sit next to everyone.

✳ ✳ ✳

Brunettes hate watching their weight.
When they get on a scale, it says, "Ouch!"

✳ ✳ ✳

The brunette bought a talking scale.
When she got on, it shouted, "Get the hell off!"

✳ ✳ ✳

When brunettes take a shower, their feet don't get wet.

✳ ✳ ✳

When the brunette tried to fly to New York, her flight got canceled.
She was so heavy the plane couldn't get off the ground.

✳ ✳ ✳

When does a brunette dress in white?
When she's dating the Stay Puft Marshmallow Man.

* * *

Brunettes are like bowling shoes.
You never know what's been in them.

* * *

Why don't brunettes wear fur coats?
They'd drive an entire species to extinction.

* * *

When brunettes walk down the street, they have to wear signs saying, "Caution: wide turns!"

* * *

A brunette prostitute mistook a Salvation Army man for a soldier and propositioned him. The Salvation Army member said, "Ma'am, you may be forgiven, as a pitiable victim of circumstances. Tell me, are you familiar with the concept of 'original sin'?"

The prostitute replied, "Well, maybe and maybe not. But if it's 'really' original, it'll cost you an extra $20."

* * *

What do brunettes call a refrigerator?
The lunchbox.

* * *

Then there was the brunette that wore an *X-Files* T-shirt.
A flying saucer landed on her.

* * *

This guy is in a bar and gets hit on by a horny brunette.

"Say, you want to have a good time? I live just a block away."

"Sure," he says, and they were off to her place.

She takes off her clothes, and he keeps staring at her. She says, "What? Is this the first pussy you've seen since you crawled out of one?"

The guy says, "No, just the first one I've seen big enough to crawl back into."

* * *

Brunettes are like vacuum cleaners.
They suck, they blow, and they get laid in closets.

* * *

It's tough being a brunette.
*Your weight has more digits than your
phone number.*

* * *

What did the brunette name her watch dogs?
Rolex and Timex.

* * *

What's the first thing a brunette hears in
the morning?
"See ya . . . ."

* * *

One brunette took up three pages in her high
school yearbook.

* * *

Brunettes are like bowling balls.
They get fingered and come back for more.

* * *

Brunettes are like shotguns.
Two cocks and they're loaded.

* * *

A furrier from the U.S. goes to Helsinki, Finland to buy furs. He arranges for a brunette to be sent to his room. When they're done, he says, "I'm afraid my Finnish isn't too good."

The brunette replies, "Your foreplay's not all that hot, either."

* * *

Why don't brunettes wear red?
Kids run up and shout, "Kool-Aid! Kool-Aid!"

* * *

One poor brunette was diagnosed with a flesh-eating bacteria.
Her doctor gave her sixty-four years to live.

* * *

Why do surfers love brunettes?
They can slap their butts and ride the waves.

* * *

The brunette took her dress to the dry cleaner and was told, "Sorry, we don't do curtains."

* * *

One time, a brunette went on a cruise.
    Whales circled the ship and sang, "We Are Family . . ."

* * *

A Chinese businessman from Hong Kong picks up a brunette in a Vegas casino and they go to his room for the evening. Once in the room they undress, climb into bed, and go at it. When finished, the Chinese man jumps up, runs over to the window, takes a deep breath, dives under the bed, climbs out the other side, jumps back into bed with the brunette, and commences to repeat the performance. The brunette is impressed with the gusto of the second encounter. When finished, the Chinese man jumps up again, runs back over to the window, takes another deep breath, dives back under the bed, climbs out the other side, jumps back into bed with the brunette, and starts again. The brunette is amazed as this sequence is repeated four times. During the fifth encore, she decides to try it herself. So when they are done, she jumps up, goes to the window and takes a deep breath of fresh air, dives under the bed . . . and finds four Chinese men.

* * *

What make-up is most used by brunettes?
"Why Bother."

* * *

Why don't brunettes get acne?
It slides off.

* * *

Why don't brunettes get liposuction?
It takes three years.

* * *

What do brunettes get in restaurants?
Estimates.

* * *

Then there was the guy who took his brunette wife
everywhere.
That way he didn't have to kiss her goodbye.

* * *

A brunette I know quit her job the other day.
It was interfering with her drinking.

* * *

Brunette: "What do you love most, my natural
beauty or my body?"
Boyfriend: "Your sense of humor."

✳ ✳ ✳

A man finds himself staying in a Vegas hotel room while on a business trip. Not wishing to be alone, he calls an "escort" service for some company. Soon, a strikingly beautiful brunette arrives. Without hesitating, the brunette says, "I want to tell you right up-front, my minimum fee is $500, and that's for a hand job."

"$500 for a hand job? Why, that's outrageous!" the man exclaimed. "No hand job in the world could be worth $500!"

The brunette summons the man to the window and points down to the parking lot below. "See that cherry red Maserati down there? I own that because of what I can do with my hands."

Against his better judgment, the man pays the $500 and sure enough, the brunette sends him into utter bliss, by far the best sexual experience of his life. After he recuperates, he says to the woman, "God, that was fantastic!! How much for a blow job?"

"$2,500," the brunette replies.

"$2,500 for a blow job?" cried the astonished man. "That's way too much!"

Again the hooker summons the man to the window, this time pointing across the street. "Do you see that large medical building right off the strip there? I own that because of what I can do with my mouth."

"Oh, no," moans the man, "this is going to break me, but I just have to try it."

Once again, the brunette takes him to the edge of the universe and back, far surpassing the pleasure he received earlier, leaving him utterly drained and totally gratified.

As soon as the man can speak again, he says, "I just have to know. How much do you get for your pussy?" The brunette drags the man to the window for a third time, points and proclaims, "Do you see the MGM Grand Hotel sitting there on the corner? I could own that if I had a pussy!"

＊ ＊ ＊

Brunettes aren't quitters!
They usually get fired.

＊ ＊ ＊

Then there was the 36-24-36 brunette.
Her other arm was just as big.

＊ ＊ ＊

Why do brunettes hate going to the zoo?
Because elephants throw them peanuts.

✳ ✳ ✳

What's a brunette's favorite snack?
Wheat Thicks.

✳ ✳ ✳

Brunettes hate the beach.
Everybody screams, "Free Willie!"

✳ ✳ ✳

A guy was married to a fat, dumpy brunette. One evening, thinking he was being funny, he said to his wife, "Perhaps we should start washing your clothes in Slim Fast. Maybe it would take a few inches off of your butt!" His wife was not amused, and decided that she simply couldn't let such a comment go unpunished.

The next morning, the husband took a pair of underwear out of his drawer.

"What the hell is this?" he said to himself as a little "dust" cloud appeared when he shook them out.

"Honey," he hollered into the bathroom. "Why did you put talcum powder in my underwear?"

She replied with a snicker, "It's not talcum powder . . . it's Miracle Grow."

* * *

It was very embarrassing when the brunette went to the beach.
Greenpeace tried to tow her back out to sea.

* * *

Why do brunettes hate birthday parties?
People try and pin a tail on them.

* * *

Brunettes' brains are like the prison system.
Not enough cells per person.

* * *

Why haven't any brunettes ever gone to the moon?
It doesn't need cleaning yet.

❋ ❋ ❋

Then there was the brunette that went on so many blind dates she thought she should get a free dog.

❋ ❋ ❋

What's the difference between brunettes and pigs?
Pigs don't turn into brunettes when they drink.

❋ ❋ ❋

A man rubbed a lamp and a genie came out. The man asked to be stronger than any other man and he was given the strength to crush boulders. He asked for the world's fastest sports car, and a Ferrari appeared in front of him. He then asked to be smarter than any other man on the earth. He was turned into a brunette.

❋ ❋ ❋

"Great, just what I need," the brunette moaned as her husband brought home a new microwave oven. "One more thing that heats up instantly and goes off in twenty seconds."

✳ ✳ ✳

Two brunettes go out one weekend without their husbands. As they headed home drunk just before dawn, they felt the urge to pee. They noticed that the only place to stop was a cemetery. Scared and drunk, they stopped and decided to go there, anyway.

The first one did not have anything to wipe herself with, so she took off her panties, used them, then threw them away. The second brunette, not finding anything to use, either, thought, "I'm not getting rid of my panties." Instead, she used the ribbon of a nearby flower wreath.

The morning after, the two husbands were talking to each other on the phone, and one says to the other: "We have to be on the lookout; it seems that these two were up to no good last night My wife came home without her panties."

The other one responded: "You're lucky, mine came home with a card stuck to her butt that read, "We will never forget you."

✳ ✳ ✳

A brunette goes into the local newspaper office to see that the obituary for her recently deceased husband is published. After the editor informs her that the fee for the obituary is fifty cents a word, she pauses, reflects, and then says, "Well, then, let it read 'Bob Stevens died.'" Confounded at the woman's thrift, the editor stammers that there is a seven-word minimum for all obituaries. The woman pauses again, counts on her fingers, and replies, "In that case, make it 'Bob Stevens died: 1983 pickup for sale.'"

✳ ✳ ✳

A guy enters a bar carrying an alligator. He says to the patrons, "Here's a deal. I'll open this alligator's mouth and put my dick inside. The gator will close his mouth for one minute, then open it, and I'll remove my unit unscathed. If it works, everyone buys me drinks."

The crowd agrees. The guy drops his pants and puts his privates in the gator's mouth. The gator closes its mouth. After a minute, the guy grabs a beer bottle and bangs the gator on the top of its head. The gator opens wide, and he removes his dick unscathed. Everyone buys him drinks.

Then he says, "I'll pay anyone $100 who's willing to give it a try."

After some time, a brunette at the back of the

bar raises her hand. "I'll give it a try," the brunette says, "but you have to promise not to hit me on the head with the beer bottle."

✳ ✳ ✳

A brunette goes into a bar and seats herself on a stool. The bartender looks at her and says, "What'll it be, lady?"

The brunette says, "Set me up with seven whiskey shots, and make them doubles."

The bartender does this and watches the woman slug one down, then the next, then the next, and so on until all seven are gone almost as quickly as they were served. Staring in disbelief, the bartender asks why she's doing all this drinking.

"You'd drink them this fast, too, if you had what I have."

The bartender hastily asks, "What do you have, Miss?"

The brunette quickly replies, "I have a dollar."

✳ ✳ ✳

The head waiter brings the bill and the brunette is horrified to see the total: $150! She didn't expect this at all and asks the waiter, "Would you mind holding my breasts while I write the check, please?"

The head waiter is taken aback. In all his years in the job he's never been asked that before; but, always eager to please the customer, he obliges.

The brunette gets up to leave, and the waiter is still perplexed. His curiosity gets the better of him and he catches up with her at the door, "I'm sorry to bother you Miss, but I'd like to know why you asked me to do that just now."

"Oh, it's quite simple, really," she replies. "I love to have my breasts held when I'm being screwed."

✳ ✳ ✳

Seeking to embarrass the new faculty member, an attractive young brunette scholar, the "old boy network" set up a prank. There was a monthly faculty dinner and each month, one of the faculty members had to give a presentation on a preselected topic. The Dean, in on the prank, informed the brunette that this task always fell to a new faculty member when possible and that this month was therefore her turn. He also told her the topic for the month was sex.

The night of the dinner the brunette was introduced.

She stood up and said, "Gentlemen, it gives me great pleasure," and sat back down.

* * *

A brunette went to her doctor for a checkup. When asked how she got the bruises on the outside of her thighs, she explained that she got them from having sex. The doctor then told her she would have to change positions until the bruises healed. The brunette replied "Oh doctor, I can't . . . my dog's breath is awful!"

* * *

Coffee Is Better Than a Brunette Because:

Coffee doesn't complain when you put whipped cream on it.

A cup of coffee looks good in the morning.

You won't fall asleep after a cup of coffee.

You can always warm coffee up.

Coffee is cheaper.

You won't get arrested for ordering coffee at 3 a.m.

Coffee never runs out.

Coffee is out of your system by tomorrow morning.

You can make coffee as sweet as you want.

You can smoke while drinking coffee.

You can put out a cigarette in a cup of coffee.

Coffee smells and tastes good.

You can always get fresh coffee.

You can turn the pot on, leave the room, and it'll be hot when you get back.

You can always ditch a bad cup of coffee.

Coffee goes down easier.

No matter how ugly you are, you can always get a cup of coffee.

Big cup or small cup? It doesn't matter.

Your coffee doesn't talk to you.

Coffee smells good in the morning.

Coffee is good when it's cold, too.

Coffee doesn't care when you dunk things in it.

Coffee doesn't care what kind of mood you're in.

Coffee doesn't shed.

Coffee is ready in fifteen minutes or less.

You can't get a cup of coffee pregnant by putting cream in it.

Coffee doesn't mind being ground.

No matter how bad coffee is, you can always make it better.

Coffee doesn't have a time of the month—it's
   good all the time.
When coffee gets old, you can throw it away.
When you have a coffee, you don't end up with
   a pube in the back of your throat.
Coffee doesn't take up half your bed.
Coffee doesn't mind if you wake up at 3 a.m.
   and decide to have a cup.
INSTANT COFFEE!
You can have an intelligent conversation
   with coffee.
It can take up to two weeks for coffee to
   grow mold.
Your coffee won't be jealous of a larger cup.

※ ※ ※

This guy was having a drink in a bar. He noticed that
the bartender was a very sexy brunette. She came
over to chat for a bit and he said, "I bet I can keep
an eye on this drink while I go to the bathroom," as
he lay a $10 bill on the bar. She knew the bathroom
was around the corner and accepted his bet. He
removed his glass eye and took off to the john.

"Very funny," the brunette said when he
returned.

He smiled and said, "OK let's try another one."

Again, he puts a $10 bill down on the table. "I'll bet you I can bite my own ear."

She matches the $10 and watches unbelievingly as the guy removes his false teeth and clamps them down on his ear.

He grins and says, "All right, one more bet, a chance to win your money back. I bet I can make love to you so tenderly that you won't feel a thing."

Thinking this was something she knew about, the brunette took him by the hand out back behind the bar and lifted her skirt. They went to town. A few moments later, she giggled, "I can feel you."

He kept on pumping and said, "Well, win some, lose some!"

✳ ✳ ✳

A brunette and her boyfriend are out for a romantic walk along a country lane. They walk hand-in-hand and as they stroll, the guy's lustful desire rises to a peak. He is just about to get frisky when the brunette says, "I hope you don't mind, but I really do need to pee."

Slightly taken aback by this vulgarity, he replies, "OK. Why don't you go behind this hedge?"

She nods agreement and disappears behind the hedge. As he waits, he can hear the sound of her panties sliding down her voluptuous legs, and imagines what is being exposed. Unable to contain his animal thoughts a moment longer, he reaches a hand through the hedge and touches her leg. He quickly brings his hand further up her thigh, until suddenly and with great astonishment he finds himself gripping a long, thick appendage hanging between her legs.

He shouts in horror, "My God, Mary! Have you changed your sex?"

"No," the brunette replies. "I've changed my mind. I'm having a dump instead."

✳ ✳ ✳

Beer Is Better Than Brunettes Because:

You can enjoy a beer all month long.

You don't have to wine and dine beer.

Your beer will always wait patiently in the car while you play football.

When your beer goes flat, you toss it out.

Beer is never late.

A beer doesn't get jealous when you grab another beer.

Hangovers go away.

Beer labels come off without a fight.

When you go to a bar, you know you can always

pick up a beer.

Beer never has a headache.

After you've had a beer, the bottle is still worth five cents.

A beer won't get upset if you come home with another beer.

If you pour a beer right, you'll always get good head.

A beer always goes down easy.

You can have more than one beer in a night, and not feel guilty.

You can share a beer with your friends.

You always know when you're the first one to pop a beer.

Beer is always wet.

Beer doesn't demand equality.

You can have a beer in public.

A beer doesn't care when you come.

A frigid beer is a good beer.

If you change beers, you don't have to pay alimony.

You don't have to wash a beer before it tastes good.

You can't catch social diseases from a beer.

When you're interrupted by a beer, it's for a good reason.

A beer is always satisfying.

A beer gets lighter the longer you hold it.

A beer won't tell you it's pregnant for fun.

A beer doesn't have in-laws.

No matter what the package, a beer still looks good.

To cool off a beer, all you have to do is put it in the fridge.

All you have to do to get over a beer is take a leak.

Beer doesn't complain about farting.

The only thing a beer tells you is when it's time to go to the bathroom.

You are never embarrassed about the beer you bring to a party.

It's OK to leave a party with a different beer than you arrived with.

You can shoot a beer.

A beer chaser is easy to catch.

Beer doesn't grow hair where it shouldn't.

Beer doesn't care how much you earn.

Beer won't complain about your choice of vacation.

Beer doesn't care if you go to sleep right after you've had it.

Beer is happy to ride in the trunk of your car.

You never have to promise to respect a beer in the morning.

Beer never complains about the wet spot.

You can put all your old beers in one room, and they won't fight.

* * *

Being a Brunette: The Good and The Bad

The Good:

1. Happiness is only a shoe shop away.
2. If you fart, it is blamed on the nearest man.
3. It is always the man's fault if the car breaks down.
4. Chocolate can really solve problems.
5. You can end a fight by crying.
6. You have the right to be a pain every month.

The Bad:

1. You always get the blame if something goes wrong.
2. The kids always see you as the one that tells them they can't get a dog and to tidy their rooms.
3. The kitchen.
4. People annoy you at totally the wrong time with their problems.
5. The week after your period no one likes you.

* * *

The Stages of a Brunette's Love Life:

When I was 14, I hoped that one day I would have a boyfriend.

When I was 16, I got a boyfriend, but there was no passion, so I decided I needed a passionate guy with a zest for life.

In college, I dated a passionate guy, but he was too emotional. Everything was an emergency, he was a drama queen, cried all the time, and threatened suicide. So I decided I needed a boy with stability.

When I was 25, I found a very stable guy, but he was boring. He was totally predictable and never got excited about anything. Life became so dull that I decided I needed a boy with some excitement.

When I was 28, I found an exciting boy, but I couldn't keep up with him. He rushed from one party to another, never settling on anything. He did mad impetuous things and flirted with everyone he met. He made me miserable as often as happy. He was great fun initially and very energetic, but directionless. So I decided to find a boy with some ambition.

When I turned 31, I found a smart, ambitious boy with his feet planted firmly on the

ground, so I moved in with him. He was
so ambitious that he dumped me and took
everything I owned.

I am older now and am looking for a guy with a
very big dick.

Redhead
Jokes

How do you know you've satisfied a redhead?
She unties you.

* * *

How do you know your first date with a redhead is
going well?
You ask her to dance and she gets on the table.

* * *

How do you know a redhead's tough?
She kick-starts her vibrator.

* * *

How do you know a redhead's really tough?
She rolls her own tampons.

* * *

How can you tell a redhead's really, really tough?
She rolls her tampons out of burlap.

* * *

What's the difference between having a job and marrying a redhead?
After ten years, the job still sucks.

* * *

Why do redheads love to masturbate?
It's sex with someone they love.

* * *

What do redheads and sperm have in common?
They both have a one in a million chance of becoming a human being.

* * *

A guy is riding down the highway on his motorcycle when he gets pulled over by a cop.

"Was I speeding, officer?" The biker asks.

"No, sir, you weren't," replies the cop.

"Then why did you pull me over?"

"That redhead you had with you fell off a mile back."

"Oh, thank God! I thought I was going deaf!"

* * *

Why do redheads like getting lots of e-mail?
They love having their mailboxes filled.

* * *

Why do redheads have clear consciences?
They've never been used.

* * *

Why do redheads rub their eyes when they wake up?
They don't have balls to scratch.

* * *

What do you call a redhead in handcuffs?
Trustworthy.

* * *

Why don't sharks eat redheads?
Professional courtesy.

✳ ✳ ✳

How do you know a redhead is cheating on you?
You buy a used car and one of her dresses is in the back seat.

✳ ✳ ✳

How many redheads does it take to screw in a light bulb?
One—she holds the bulb while the world revolves around her.

✳ ✳ ✳

What does a redhead say to her husband after sex?
"I'll be home in twenty minutes."

✳ ✳ ✳

How do you paralyze a redhead from the waist down?
Marry her.

✳ ✳ ✳

Why do men cheat on redheads?
So they can be on top.

* * *

How did the redhead meet her husband?
They were dating the same woman.

* * *

What do you call it when a redhead talks dirty to
a man?
$3.99 a minute.

* * *

Why did the man not talk to his redheaded wife for
eighteen months?
He didn't want to interrupt.

* * *

How do you make a redhead scream twice?
Fuck her in the ass then wipe off on her curtains.

* * *

How do you stop a redhead from drowning?
Shoot her before she hits the water.

* * *

What's brown and black and looks good on
a redhead?
A Doberman.

* * *

What's the difference between a vampire and
a redhead?
A vampire only sucks your blood at night.

* * *

A terrorist hijacked a plane full of redheads.
*He threatened to release one per hour if his
demands weren't met.*

* * *

What's the difference between a redhead and a catfish?
One is a scum-sucking bottom feeder. The other is just a fish.

* * *

How is a redhead like a grapefruit?
They both squirt when you eat them.

* * *

What's the difference between a penis and a paycheck?
You don't have to beg a redhead to blow your paycheck.

* * *

What did the redheaded broker's wife say when he caught her cheating on him?
"Sorry, dear. I've gone public!"

* * *

How do you know a redhead has been using your computer?
There's an ax sticking out of your monitor.

* * *

Why are sheep better than redheads?
Sheep don't talk.

* * *

What's the best thing about getting a blow job from a redhead?
Ten minutes of silence.

* * *

How are redheads like tampons?
They both come with strings attached.

* * *

A blonde, a redhead, and a brunette are sinking in a boat. Who gets saved?
The American male.

✳ ✳ ✳

What's the difference between a dog and
a redhead?
*After you've had it a year, the dog is still glad to
see you.*

✳ ✳ ✳

Why do redheads like men with earrings?
They've experienced pain and bought jewelry.

✳ ✳ ✳

A P.E.T.A. member sees a redhead wearing a fur
coat. He strides up to her and asks, "Do you know
how many animals had to die to make that coat?"
    She snaps back, "Do you know how many
animals I had to fuck to get this coat?"

✳ ✳ ✳

How do redheads say, "Fuck you?"
"Trust me."

✳ ✳ ✳

Why do redheads really hate blow jobs?
*They're afraid they'll interfere with their
unemployment benefits.*

✳ ✳ ✳

If Tarzan and Jane were redheads, what would
Cheetah be?
A fur coat.

✳ ✳ ✳

What do you get when you cross a redhead and
a Mac?
A computer that never goes down.

✳ ✳ ✳

What do you get when you cross a redhead and
a PC?
A fucking know-it-all.

✳ ✳ ✳

What's the difference between a redhead and a bowl of Jell-O?
Jell-O shakes when you eat it.

* * *

What's the difference between a redhead and the Bermuda Triangle?
The Bermuda Triangle swallows seamen.

* * *

What does a redhead hate most about having a colostomy?
Trying to find shoes that match the bag.

* * *

Why are redheads prone to crow's feet?
From saying, "Suck what?"

* * *

Why do redheads close their eyes when screwing?
So they can pretend they're shopping.

* * *

What's the difference between a redhead and
a canoe?
Canoes tip.

* * *

What's the difference between a redhead and
a barracuda?
Nail polish.

* * *

What do you call a redhead's nipple?
The tip of the iceberg.

* * *

What's a redhead's biggest lie?
"It's only a cold sore."

* * *

What does a redhead do with her asshole in
the morning?

She sends him off to work.

✳ ✳ ✳

What's the difference between a redhead and a
toilet seat?
Toilet seats warm up when you touch them.

✳ ✳ ✳

A redhead is walking down the street and is
approached by a panhandler.
　　"I haven't eaten in three weeks," he whines.
　　"Wow! I wish I had your willpower!" she replies.

✳ ✳ ✳

What do you get when you come in a redhead?
Ice cream.

✳ ✳ ✳

What's the difference between a redhead and a
block of ice?
In time, ice melts.

* * *

What's the most common STD among redheads?
Headaches.

* * *

Why don't redheads exercise?
If God had meant for them to bend over, he would have put diamonds on the floor.

* * *

What did the redhead do when she met a man with a heart of gold?
She ripped it out and sold it.

* * *

How does a redhead abuse her husband?
She stays married to him.

* * *

Why do divorces from redheads cost so much?
They're worth it.

＊ ＊ ＊

How did the redhead commit suicide?
She piled up all her clothes and jumped.

＊ ＊ ＊

How is a redhead like a defense contractor?
They both charge $100 per screw.

＊ ＊ ＊

Why is a redhead like a movie theater?
You pay before you enter.

＊ ＊ ＊

What do you call a redhead who moans and shudders and cries out during sex?
Hypocrite.

＊ ＊ ＊

Why is hiring a redhead like buying a house?
You need a large down payment.

❋ ❋ ❋

Why do redheads like rodeo riders?
They only stay on for eight seconds.

❋ ❋ ❋

Why was the expensive redheaded call girl
nicknamed "Federal Express?"
*She was absolutely, positively guaranteed to be
there overnight.*

❋ ❋ ❋

Why are redheads like screen doors?
*They both loosen up after you bang them a
few times.*

❋ ❋ ❋

A redhead is sitting at a bar and gets approached
by a male patron.

"Miss, do you think you could love me?"

"I'm sorry, but my heart belongs to another," she
replied, "but the rest of me is up for auction."

✳ ✳ ✳

Why do redheads do it doggie-style?
They hate seeing a man have a good time.

✳ ✳ ✳

A redhead goes to see a fortune-teller.

"I'm sorry," says the fortune-teller, "but your husband will soon die a very violent death."

"Oh?" asked the redhead. "Will I be acquitted?"

✳ ✳ ✳

Blonde: "Do you talk to your husband during sex?"
Redhead: "Sure, if there's a phone around."

✳ ✳ ✳

Why is a redhead like a tampon?
They're both stuck up cunts.

✳ ✳ ✳

What's the difference between poverty and
a redhead?
Poverty sucks.

* * *

What does a redhead do when she climaxes?
Drops her gun.

* * *

How can you tell a redhead is having her period?
You can't. She has PMS every day.

* * *

What's a redhead's idea of safe sex?
No cameras around.

* * *

Where does a redhead hide a dead body?
In the chili.

* * *

What's the difference between a redhead and the IRS?
When a redhead catches you cheating, she stops screwing you.

* * *

What's the difference between a redhead and a pit bull?
The pantsuit.

* * *

What's the difference between a vulture and a redhead?
A vulture waits until you're dead to eat your heart out.

* * *

Why does it take four redheads with PMS to screw in a light bulb?
IT JUST DOES, OK?

* * *

Why are redheads like pay toilets?
They're either taken or full of shit.

* * *

What's the difference between a redhead and a killer whale?
Killer whales eat seamen.

* * *

Why are volcanoes better than redheads?
They never fake eruptions.

* * *

A ravishing redhead strolls into a bar wearing the tightest jeans a male patron had ever seen. Fascinated, he sidles over to her and asks," How do you get into those pants?"

   "Well, you could start by buying me a drink."

* * *

Why do redheads prefer sex to bowling?
*The balls are lighter and you don't need
special shoes.*

* * *

How are an oven and a redhead alike?
*You have to get them hot before you stick the
meat in.*

* * *

The doctor comes into the office and announces to
the man, I'm sorry, you have got the clap!"
   He dashes out in rage and goes down to the
street corner and confronts the redheaded hooker
working there. "You gave me the clap, you bitch."
   "No, I didn't," replied the hooker. "You bought it."

* * *

Redheads are like stale beer.
You won't get head from either one.

* * *

What is a redhead's favorite drink?
The next one.

* * *

What do you call a blonde, a brunette, and a redhead together?
See no evil. Hear no evil. Evil.

* * *

A couple was in the marriage counselor's office.

"I'm a sucker for redheads," explained the man. "I met my wife and fell in love with those long red locks. It was a whirlwind romance and we were married the next day. The morning after, I was half-asleep and left a twenty on the nightstand."

"Well, these things happen," soothes the counselor.

"Yes, but then she mumbled, 'You owe me another twenty, needle-dick!'"

* * *

Why wouldn't the redhead take a blood test?
She didn't want another prick.

* * *

Why do redheads like soybeans?
They're the perfect meat substitute.

* * *

Why do redheads suck on ice cubes?
So they can cold-cock their next customer.

* * *

Where do redheaded pilots sit?
In the cuntpit.

* * *

Why are redheaded nymphomaniacs so smart?
They're always thinking hard.

* * *

Where do redheads keep their addresses?
In a little black-and-blue book.

* * *

How much do you pay a redhead for a golden shower?
The going rate.

* * *

What kind of notes do redheaded dominatrixes send?
Chain letters.

* * *

Why don't redheads accept dinner invitations?
They're tied up most every night.

* * *

How do you stop a redhead from fucking you?
Marry her.

* * *

How do you tickle a redhead?
Gucci, Gucci goo.

* * *

What do redheads make for dinner?
Reservations.

* * *

How do redheads wean their young?
Fire the maid.

* * *

How do you tell the redhead in a Chinese restaurant?
She's the one not sharing the food.

* * *

How do redheads engage in oral sex?
They yell, "Fuck you!"

* * *

How does a redhead call her family for dinner?
"Everybody in the car!"

* * *

Why do redheads love prostitution?
You got it, you sell it, you still got it.

✳ ✳ ✳

Why did the redhead call her husband a
hobosexual?
He was a bum fuck.

✳ ✳ ✳

Why did God give redheads nipples?
To make suckers out of men.

✳ ✳ ✳

A blonde, a brunette, and a redhead are vying for
the same promotion, so the boss devises a test. He
places $500 on the desk of each woman while they
are at lunch.

The blonde returns it to him right away.

The brunette invests it and returns $1000 the
next day.

The redhead keeps it and says nothing.

Who gets the promotion?

The one with the big tits.

✳ ✳ ✳

What did the redhead say when her daughter wanted to go out to play?
"Shut-up and deal!"

✳ ✳ ✳

What did the redhead say when her son said, "I hate Daddy?"
"Then just eat your vegetables."

✳ ✳ ✳

What's the difference between a redhead and a prostitute?
Prostitutes don't drive Ferraris.

✳ ✳ ✳

How many redheads does it take to screw in a light bulb?
Five. Four to bitch about it and one to nag her boyfriend to do it.

✳ ✳ ✳

What's 10, 9, 8, 7, 6, 5.4.3.2.1?
A redhead getting older.

* * *

Science has discovered a food that reduces a
redhead's sex drive by 90%.
Wedding cake.

* * *

A guy sidles up to a redhead in a bar.
     "I'm ten-inches long and three-inches thick," he
brags. "Interested?"
     "Fascinated," she replied, "And how big is
your dick?"

* * *

What's the difference between a redhead and
a computer?
A computer will take a three-inch floppy.

* * *

How is a redhead like a condom?
They both spend most of their time in your wallet.

＊ ＊ ＊

How do redheads sleep?
First, they lie on one side, then they lie on the other.

＊ ＊ ＊

How do you define "tragedy"?
A bus full of redheads going over a cliff with three empty seats.

＊ ＊ ＊

Why are redheads like bumper stickers?
Both are hard to get off.

＊ ＊ ＊

Don't get married.
Just find a redhead you hate and buy her a house.

＊ ＊ ＊

What do you call a redhead who doesn't cause pain
and agony?
Unemployed.

＊ ＊ ＊

What did the redhead do when her boyfriend said
she needed to be more affectionate?
She got two more boyfriends.

＊ ＊ ＊

Then there was the redhead who had a wet dream.
She dreamed she won a case of beer.

＊ ＊ ＊

Why do redheads have two sets of lips?
So they can piss and moan at the same time.

＊ ＊ ＊

How are redheads like crime?
Neither one pays.

＊ ＊ ＊

Why are there so many single redheads?
They haven't met Dr. Right.

* * *

Why should redheads be buried twelve feet in the ground?
Because deep down, they're good.

* * *

What do you get a redhead for her twenty-first birthday?
Bail.

* * *

Why are redheads like laxatives?
They irritate the shit out of you.

* * *

What's six inches long, two inches wide and drives redheads wild?
Money.

* * *

"How come you never tell me when you have an orgasm?" a guy asked his redheaded lover.
"Because you're never around when I do."

* * *

What's the difference between a redhead and a can of tuna?
It doesn't take five beers to open a can of tuna.

* * *

Why are there two million abused redheads in the United States?
They never shut the fuck up!

* * *

What do you call a redhead with PMS and ESP?
A bitch who knows everything.

* * *

What sport do redheads like to watch most?
Cockfighting.

* * *

What do redheads and vegetarians have in common?
They don't eat meat.

* * *

A redhead goes to see her gynecologist, who also happens to be a redhead.

"I have good news and bad news," says the doctor.

"What's the bad news?"

"You're showing signs of becoming a lesbian."

"And the good news?"

"I think you're cute."

* * *

How is a redhead like a car engine?
*On a really cold morning, when you really need it,
it won't turn over.*

* * *

Why do husbands of redheads die young?
They want to.

* * *

What's the difference between a redhead and
a terrorist?
Terrorists have fewer demands.

* * *

Never use a redheaded cab driver.
You'll get tied-up in traffic.

* * *

Why do redheads love being taken to restaurants?
They love whining and dining.

* * *

How can you tell if a redhead is horny?
Check which end of her broomstick she's riding.

* * *

How is a redhead like a bank CD?
They both penalize you for early withdrawal.

* * *

Why couldn't the redheaded singer finish a song?
She kept passing out after the first eight bars.

* * *

Only two percent of redheaded secretaries are touch typists.
The rest are hunt'n'peckers.

* * *

What's the mating call of the redhead?
"NEXT!"

* * *

How does a redhead part her hair?
She spreads her legs.

* * *

How can you tell a redhead has reached orgasm?
The batteries die.

* * *

How do you drown a redhead?
Put a mirror on the bottom of the pool.

* * *

How do you describe a redhead surrounded by drooling idiots?
Flattered.

* * *

What's the best redheaded secretary to have?
One that never misses a period.

* * *

What do you call a redhead without an asshole?
Divorced.

✳ ✳ ✳

What should you give a man who has everything?
A redhead to show him how to use it.

✳ ✳ ✳

What do a redhead and a department store have in common?
Men's pants, half-off.

✳ ✳ ✳

Why is beer better than a redhead?
A frigid beer is a good beer.

✳ ✳ ✳

Why is a redhead like a freight train?
You can hear 'em coming a mile away.

✳ ✳ ✳

How did the redhead know when she was going to die?
The warden told her.

* * *

What's the difference between a redhead and a freezer?
You have to plug in a freezer.

* * *

What does a redhead say as she's reaching orgasm?
"I have to hang up now, Mom . . ."

* * *

Why is a redhead like a diaper?
They're both always on your ass and full of crap.

* * *

Then there was the redheaded nymphomaniac . . .
She needed a man at least once a month.

* * *

Why do redheads use tampons instead of sanitary napkins?
Nothing goes in without a string attached.

* * *

How do you spot a sadistic redhead?
She does nice things for masochists.

* * *

Then there was the redhead who slept with her brother-in-law.
She had it in for her sister.

* * *

What does a redhead say at an orgy?
"What? My turn again?"

* * *

How does a redhead do aerobics?
She shops faster.

* * *

What's the difference between happiness and
a redhead?
Money can't buy happiness.

* * *

Why do redheads prefer cucumbers to men?
They stay hard the whole week.

* * *

What's the difference between a redhead and
a pothole?
You swerve to avoid a pothole.

* * *

What do you call a redhead that uses the pill?
Humanitarian.

* * *

What's the definition of a redhead who just left
the room?
Fucking bitch.

* * *

Why do redheads throw away their garbage in clear
plastic bags?
So brunettes can go window shopping.

* * *

What's the difference between a blonde and
a redhead?
A blonde gets real orgasms and phony diamonds.

* * *

How do you know a redhead is Catholic?
When she goes to confession, she brings a lawyer.

* * *

Then there was the redheaded hooker that served
sadists.
She was strapped for cash.

* * *

How do you know a redhead is having an orgasm?
She drops her briefcase.

* * *

Then there was the redhead who ate in a Chinese-German restaurant.
An hour later she was hungry for power.

* * *

Then there was the redheaded nymphomaniac.
She had sex after having her hair done.

* * *

How can you tell there's a blonde at a cockfight?
She enters a parrot.

* * *

How can you tell a brunette is at the cockfight?
She bets on the parrot.

✳ ✳ ✳

How can you tell there's a redhead at the cockfight?
The parrot wins.

✳ ✳ ✳

Why do redheads fake orgasms?
Because men fake foreplay.

✳ ✳ ✳

What do you call twenty skydiving redheads?
Skeet.

✳ ✳ ✳

What do you call a redhead "working" the interstate?
A tollhouse cookie.

✳ ✳ ✳

What's cold and smokes like a chimney?
A redhead.

* * *

What do redheads give the blind for Christmas?
A paint-by-numbers set.

* * *

Then there was the redhead that booked two
"clients" at the same time.
She managed to squeeze them both in.

* * *

What do you call ten redheads in a freezer?
Cold cunts.

* * *

Why are redheads like elephants?
Neither one ever forgets.

* * *

What's the difference between a redhead and
taxes?
Taxes suck.

＊ ＊ ＊

How are redheads like parole officers?
Neither one ever lets you finish a sentence.

＊ ＊ ＊

What's a redhead's idea of doggie-style?
Rolling over and playing dead.

＊ ＊ ＊

What do you call a redhead with two daughters?
Madam.

＊ ＊ ＊

Why did the redhead stop selling blow jobs and become a computer programmer?
Less down time.

＊ ＊ ＊

What do you call a redhead on a water bed?
Lake Placid.

* * *

Then there was the redhead who became a
practical nurse.
She married a wealthy old patient.

* * *

What does a redhead give a man who has
everything?
Encouragement.

* * *

Give a redhead twelve inches and she thinks she's
a ruler.

* * *

Did you hear about the guy who chased a redhead
for three years?
He had to marry her for his money.

* * *

Then there was the redhead who made it in Hollywood the hard way.
She had talent.

* * *

What does a redhead like better than roses on her piano?
Two lips on her organ.

* * *

Why are redheads like pianos?
When they aren't upright, they're grand.

* * *

Who invented the Limbo?
A redhead sneaking under a pay toilet door.

* * *

What's black-and-blue and lies on the sidewalk?
A guy who tells too many redheaded jokes.

* * *

How does a redhead lube her car?
She runs over a brunette.

* * *

What does a redhead serve at a party?
Chips and dips and chains and whips.

* * *

Why did the redhead enjoy being a hermit?
She liked going off by herself.

* * *

Why do redheads like Valentine's Day?
Their men all have a heart on.

* * *

Why did the redhead think other people thought her husband was a pauper?
She hears everybody say "That poor man . . ."

* * *

What's safer, a redhead or a piranha?
A piranha. They only attack in schools.

* * *

How to you change a redhead's mood?
Wait ten seconds.

* * *

What's a redhead's dating philosophy?
The way to a man's heart is through his rib cage.

* * *

What's the difference between a redhead and
a Nazi?
There are some people who like Nazis.

* * *

Why is it better to date a blonde than a redhead?
You can ignore a blonde safely.

* * *

Why is it better to date a blonde than a redhead?
Blondes don't carry their attorney's phone number on them.

✳ ✳ ✳

Why is it better to fuck a blonde than a redhead?
You'll be able to find your wallet in the morning.

✳ ✳ ✳

Why is it better to date a blonde than a redhead?
Blondes don't think they are entitled to a free ride.

✳ ✳ ✳

What is the difference between sticking your hand in a blender and a redhead?
There's a 50/50 chance the blender isn't on.

✳ ✳ ✳

What's the difference between a redhead and a lawyer?
There are some ways a lawyer won't screw you.

* * *

How does a redhead change a light bulb?
She bitches 'til you do it.

* * *

How do you start an argument with a redhead?
Say something.

* * *

What do you get when you cross a redhead, a
battery and a potato chip?
A redhead who's Eveready and Frito-Lay.

* * *

How can you tell a man has a redheaded girlfriend?
Check his butt for a brand.

* * *

A redhead walks into a pharmacy and asks the clerk
if they sell extra large condoms.

"Yes, we do," replied the clerk. "Would you like

to buy some?"

"No, I'll just wait around until someone does."

✳ ✳ ✳

How do you remember a redhead's birthday?
Forget it once.

✳ ✳ ✳

What's the difference between a blonde and
a redhead?
A redhead is a blonde from Hell.

✳ ✳ ✳

What do you call a man with a redhead?
Hostage.

✳ ✳ ✳

What do redheads think of al-Qaeda?
Amateurs!

✳ ✳ ✳

What's a redhead's idea of natural childbirth?
No makeup.

* * *

What did the blind redhead say when she made love to a guy named Cohen?
"Funny, you don't feel Jewish."

* * *

Did you hear about the new redhead disease?
It's called MAIDS. If they don't get one, they die.

* * *

Why do redheads hate 69?
The lousy view.

* * *

What does a redhead scream when climaxing?
Her own name.

* * *

Why was the redhead so embarrassed at the airport?
Her Ben-Wa balls set off the metal detector.

* * *

A man asked his redheaded date, "Do you smoke after sex?"
"I don't know. I never looked."

* * *

Why do redheads have big tits and tight pussies?
Men have big mouths and little pricks.

* * *

How is a redhead like a bank?
When you withdraw your assets, she loses interest.

* * *

What do you call a beautiful, big-breasted redhead?
Bitch.

* * *

Why do dogs stick their noses in redheads' crotches?
Because they can.

* * *

Why is a convict just before sentencing like an inexperienced redhead?
They both know it will be hard, but they don't know for how long.

* * *

How can you tell a disadvantaged redhead?
She drives a domestic car.

* * *

Why did the producer ask the redhead to take off her clothes?
He wanted to see if she could make it big.

* * *

Why do redheads like doing it doggie-style?
So they can watch Home Shopping Network.

* * *

Why did the redhead sleep with the judge?
To get an honorable discharge.

* * *

Why are there so few redheaded alcoholics?
Booze kills the pain.

* * *

How can you tell if a redhead is a bitch?
She's breathing.

* * *

How can you tell a redhead's a bitch?
She's too good to go fuck herself.

* * *

Then there was the redheaded divorce lawyer who
sent out 3,000 valentines signed "Guess Who?"

* * *

Why do redheads hate pornography?
It gives them eyestrain.

* * *

Then there was the redhead that got a set of golf clubs for her husband.
What a trade!

* * *

What did the redhead do when her son wanted to play with Rover?
She dug him up.

* * *

How is a redhead like a tennis racquet?
They're both high-strung.

* * *

What did the redheaded doctor do when her patient was at death's door?
She pulled him through.

✳ ✳ ✳

A man calls his redheaded waitress over.

"Miss, this apple pie is smashed!"

"Well, when you ordered, you told me to step on it."

✳ ✳ ✳

What musical do redheads hate?
Ragtime.

✳ ✳ ✳

Why do redheads like cars with small steering wheels?
So they can drive with their handcuffs on.

✳ ✳ ✳

A man says to his redheaded wife, "Tomorrow is our twentieth anniversary. What would you like?"

"Well," she mused, "I'd like to go somewhere I've never been before."

"Try the kitchen."

∗ ∗ ∗

Then there was the redhead who saved up for years to buy a house.
The vice squad wouldn't let her run it.

∗ ∗ ∗

A kid comes home from school and says to his redheaded mom, "Mom I've got a problem."

Red says, "Tell me."

He tells her that the boys at school are using two words he doesn't understand.

She asks him what are they.

He says, "Well, pussy and bitch."

The mom says, "Oh that's no big deal. Pussy is a cat like our little Mittens, and bitch is a female dog like our Sandy."

He thanks her and goes to visit his dad in the workshop in the basement.

He says to his dad, "Dad, the boys at school are using words I don't know, and I asked mom and I don't think she told me the exact meaning."

Dad says, "Son, I told you never to go to mom with these matters. She can't handle them. What are the words?"

The son tells him, "'pussy' and 'bitch.'"

Dad says, "OK," and pulls a *Playboy* down from the shelf, takes a marker and circles the pubic area of the centerfold and says, "Son, everything inside this circle, is pussy."

"OK, Dad, so what's a 'bitch'?"

"Son," he says, "everything outside that circle."

* * *

What do you say to a redhead that won't give in?
"Have another beer."

* * *

Difference between a man buying a lottery ticket and a man fighting with a redhead?
The man has a chance at winning at the lottery.

* * *

What's the difference between a prostitute, a nymphomaniac, and a redhead?

The prostitute says, "Aren't you done yet?"

The nympho says, "Are you done already?"

The redhead says, "Beige . . . I think I'll paint the ceiling beige."

＊ ＊ ＊

What do a bowling ball and a redhead have
in common?
Chances are they'll both end up in the gutter.

＊ ＊ ＊

Person 1: What's the difference between a redhead
and garbage?

Person 2: Garbage gets taken out at least once
a week.

Person 1: Wrong. You tie the garbage up before
you take it out.

＊ ＊ ＊

What do you call a basement full of redheads?
A whine cellar.

＊ ＊ ＊

What do you call an unmarried redhead in a BMW?
Divorcée

＊ ＊ ＊

What's the most important thing a redhead asks her date?
"Are you paying by the act or by the hour?"

* * *

Only two things are necessary to keep a redhead happy.
One is to let her think she is having her own way, and the other is to let her have it.

* * *

What's the true definition of a redhead?
A blonde with the fire of passion.

* * *

What's the difference between a blonde and a redhead in bed?
A blonde lets you leave the bed when you are satisfied, while a redhead lets you leave the bed when SHE is satisfied.

* * *

What do you get when you cross Raggedy Ann with the Pillsbury Doughboy?
An angry redhead with a yeast infection.

✳ ✳ ✳

A man doing market research knocked on a door and was greeted by a redhead with three small children running around at her feet.

He said, "I'm doing some research for Vaseline. Have you ever used the product?"

She said, "Yes. My husband and I use it all the time."

"And if you don't mind me asking, what do you use it for?"

"We use it for sex."

The researcher was a little taken aback.

He said, "Usually people lie to me and say that they use it on a child's bicycle chain or to help with a gate hinge. But, in fact, I know that most people do use it for sex. I admire you for your honesty. Since you've been frank so far, can you tell me exactly how you use it for sex?"

The redhead said, "I don't mind telling you at all. My husband and I put it on the door knob and it keeps the kids out."

✳ ✳ ✳

What's the difference between a redhead and a
Doberman pinscher?
Some people actually like Dobermans.

✳ ✳ ✳

Why do redheads think they're special?
*It's amazing what arrogance and a lack of
sensitivity will do for your ego.*

✳ ✳ ✳

Red on the head, fire in the hole . . . .

✳ ✳ ✳

A highway patrolman was rushed to the hospital
with an inflamed appendix. The doctors operated
and advised him that all was well. However, the
patrolman kept feeling something pulling at the hairs
in his crotch. Worried, he finally got enough energy
to pull his hospital gown up enough so he could
look at what was making him so uncomfortable.
Taped firmly across his pubic hair were three

wide strips of adhesive tape, the kind that takes everything with it when you pull it off.

Written in large black letters across the tape was the sentence: "Get well quick—from the redhead nurse you gave a ticket to last week."

* * *

A redhead who was leaving her cheating husband spent the first day packing her belongings. On the second day, she had the movers come and collect her things. On the third day, she sat down for the last time at their beautiful dining room table, put on some soft background music, and feasted on a pound of shrimp, a jar of caviar and a bottle of chardonnay. When she had finished, she went into each and every room and stuffed half-eaten shrimp shells dipped in caviar into the hollow of all of the curtain rods. She then cleaned up the kitchen and left.

When the husband returned with his new girlfriend, all was bliss for the first few days. Then, slowly, the house began to smell. They tried everything: cleaning, mopping and airing the place out. Vents were checked for dead rodents, carpets were steam-cleaned and air fresheners were hung everywhere! Exterminators were brought in. In the end they even paid to replace the expensive wool carpeting. Nothing worked. People stopped coming over to visit. Repairmen refused to work in the house. Finally, they could not take the stench any longer and decided to move. A month later, even though they had cut their price in half, they could not find a buyer for their stinky house. Finally, they had to borrow a huge sum of money from the bank to purchase a new place.

The ex-wife called the man and asked how things were going. He told her the saga of the rotting house. She listened politely and said that she missed her old home terribly and would be willing to reduce her divorce settlement in exchange for getting the house back. Knowing his ex-wife had no idea how bad the smell was, he agreed on a price that was about 1/10 of what the house had been worth, but only if she were to sign the papers that very day. She agreed, and within the hour his lawyers delivered the paperwork. A week later, the man and his girlfriend stood smiling as they watched the moving company pack everything to take to their new home, including the curtain rods.

* * *

The genie tells a redhead she can have two wishes—provided that her husband gets double.

She thinks for a moment about her worthless husband and then says, "OK, give me ten million dollars and beat me half-to-death."

✳ ✳ ✳

A redhead goes on vacation to the Caribbean.

Upon arriving, she meets a black man, and after a night of passionate lovemaking she asks him, "What is your name?"

"I can't tell you," the black man says.

Every night they meet and every night she asks him again what his name is and he always responds the same—he can't tell her.

On her last night there the redhead asks again, "Can you please tell me your name?"

"I can't because you will laugh at me," the black man says. "There is no reason for me to laugh at you," the redhead says.

"Fine, my name is Snow," the black man replies. The redhead bursts into laughter, and the black man gets mad and says, "I knew you would make fun of it."

The redhead replies, "I'm not making fun of you. I'm thinking of my husband who won't believe me when I tell him I had ten inches of Snow everyday in the Caribbean!"

* * *

A husband that was completely whipped by his redheaded wife complained to his psychiatrist. The psychiatrist advised him to assert himself more.

"You don't have to let your wife bully you," the shrink said. "Now, go home and show her you're the boss."

The husband decided to take the doctor's advice. He went home, slammed the door, shook his fist in his wife's face, and growled, "From now on you're taking orders from me! I want my dinner right now, and when you get it on the table, go upstairs and lay out my clothes. Tonight I am going out with the boys. You are going to stay at home where you belong. Another thing, you know who is going to tie my bow tie?"

"I most certainly do," said his wife, smiling sweetly. "The undertaker."

* * *

Two men were talking. One said: "I'd love to be casseroled by a redhead."

"What's that mean?" his puzzled friend asked. "Casseroled is a cooking term, meaning to be done slowly for a long time."

The first man shrugged, then replied, "Exactly."

* * *

Little Red Riding Hood is skipping down the road when she sees a big bad wolf crouched down behind a log.

"My, what big eyes you have, Mr. Wolf."

The wolf jumps up and runs away.

Further down the road, Little Red Riding Hood sees the wolf again, and this time he is crouched behind a bush.

"My, what big ears you have, Mr. Wolf."

Again, the wolf jumps up and runs away.

About two miles down the road, Little Red Riding Hood sees the wolf again, and this time he is crouched down behind a rock.

"My what big teeth you have, Mr. Wolf."

With that, the wolf jumps up and screams, "Will you knock it off? I'm trying to take a shit!"

* * *

Blonds tease, but redheads please.

* * *

A redhead walked into a drugstore and tells the pharmacist she needs some cyanide. The pharmacist said, "Why in the world do you need cyanide?"

The lady then explained she needed it to poison her husband.

The pharmacist's eyes got big and he said, "Lord have mercy, I can't give you cyanide to kill your husband! That's against the law! I'll lose my license, they'll throw both of us in jail and all kinds of bad things will happen! Absolutely not, you can NOT have any cyanide!" Then the redhead reached into her purse and pulled out a picture of her husband in bed with the pharmacist's wife. The pharmacist looked at the picture and replied, "Well, now, you didn't tell me you had a prescription."

✳ ✳ ✳

A man left for work one Friday afternoon. But it was payday, so instead of going home, he stayed out the entire weekend partying with the boys and spending his entire paycheck. When he finally appeared at home on Sunday night, he was confronted by his angry redheaded wife. She screamed at him for nearly two hours straight. Finally, the redhead stopped the screaming and said to him, "How would you like it if you didn't see ME for two or three days?"

The husband replied, "That would be fine with me."

Monday went by, and he didn't see his wife. Tuesday and Wednesday came and went with the same results. But on Thursday, the swelling went down just enough where he could see her a little out of the corner of his left eye.

✳ ✳ ✳

A couple went on vacation to a fishing resort. The husband liked to fish at the crack of dawn. The redheaded wife liked to read. One morning, the husband returned after several hours of fishing and decided to take a short nap. Although the wife wasn't familiar with the lake, she decided to take the boat. She took the boat out a short distance, anchored, and returned to reading her book.

Along came the sheriff in his boat. He pulled up alongside her and said, "Good morning, Ma'am. What are you doing?"

"Reading my book," she replied. "Isn't it obvious?"

"You're in a restricted fishing area," he informed her.

"But officer, I'm not fishing. Can't you see that?"

"Yes, but you have all the equipment. I'll have to take you in and write you up."

"If you do that, I'll have to charge you with rape," snapped the irate woman.

"But, I haven't even touched you," groused the sheriff.

"Yes, that's true," she replied, "But you do have all the equipment."

✳ ✳ ✳

Redheads are like the stock market.
They're irrational and can bankrupt you if you're not careful.

✳ ✳ ✳

Redheads are like parking meters.
If you don't feed them with enough money you face serious consequences.

✳ ✳ ✳

Redheads are like fax machines.
They're useful for one very specific purpose, but otherwise they're just high-maintenance paperweights.

* * *

What is the difference between sex with a blonde and sex with a redhead?
Blondes come with instructions.
Redheads come with spring-loaded legs.

* * *

How do you know when you've had sex with a redhead?
If you are dehydrated, can't walk, and have blood running down your back, you've been with a redhead.

* * *

A redhead walked into a bank one morning with a purse full of money. She wanted to open a savings account and insisted on talking to the president of the bank because, she said, she had a lot of money. After a long discussion, an employee took the woman to the bank president's office. The president of the bank asked her how much she wanted to deposit. She placed her purse on his desk and replied, "$165,000."

The bank president was curious and asked her how she had been able to save so much money. The woman replied that she made bets. The bank president was surprised and asked, "What kind of bets?" The woman replied, "Well, I bet you $25,000 that your testicles are square." The bank president started to laugh and told the woman that it was impossible to win a bet like that. The woman never batted an eye. She just looked at the bank president and said, "Would you like to take my bet?" "Certainly!" he replied. "I bet you $25,000 that my testicles are not square." "Done," the redhead answered. "But given the amount of money involved, if you don't mind I would like to come back at 10 o'clock tomorrow morning with my lawyer as a witness."

"No problem," said the president of the bank confidently.

That night he became very nervous about the bet and spent a long time in front of the mirror examining his testicles, turning them this way and that, checking them over again and again until he was positive that no one could consider his testicles to be square, and reassuring himself that there was no way he could lose the bet.

The next morning at exactly 10 o'clock the redhead arrived at the bank president's office with her lawyer and acknowledged the $25,000 bet made the day before about whether or not the bank president's testicles were square. The bank president confirmed that the bet was the same as the one made the day before. Then the redhead asked him to drop his pants, so that she and her lawyer could see clearly. The bank president was happy to oblige. The redhead came closer so she could see better and asked the bank president if she could touch them. "Of course," was his reply. "Given the amount of money involved, you should be 100% sure," he continued.

The redhead did so with a little smile. Suddenly, the bank president noticed that the lawyer was banging his head against the wall. He asked the redhead why the lawyer was doing that and she replied, "Oh, it's probably because I bet him $100,000 that around 10 o'clock in the morning I would be holding the balls of the president of the bank!"

✳ ✳ ✳

In a train compartment, there are three men and a ravishing redhead. The four passengers join in conversation, which very soon turns erotic.

Then, the redhead proposes, "If each of you will give me $1, I will show you my legs." The men,

charmed by this redhead, all pull a buck out of
their wallets.

And then the redhead lifts up her dress a bit to
show her legs.

Then she says, "If each of you gentlemen will
give me $10, I'll show you my thighs," and men
being what they are, they each pull out a ten dollar
bill. The redhead pulls up her dress all the way
to show her legs in full. Conversation continues,
and the men, a bit excited, have all taken off their
coats. Then the redhead says, "If you will give me
$100, I will show you where I was operated on
for appendicitis." All three fork over the money.
The redhead then turns to the window and points
outside at a building they're passing. "See there in
the distance. That's the hospital where I had
it done!"

* * *

If you love a redhead, set her free—if she follows
you everywhere you go, pitches a tent on your front
lawn and puts your new girlfriend in the hospital,
she's yours.

* * *

337

What do redheads and McDonald's have in common?
You've never had it so good and so fast.

* * *

A frustrated redhead decided her sex life needed spicing up after twenty years of marriage. After her husband went to work she slipped out, went into a lingerie shop, and picked up a pair of crotchless underwear. She went home, perfumed herself, donned the new garment, and selected a short skirt to go with it. She greeted her husband when he came home from work and sat across from him after preparing him a drink. She slowly spread her legs, and in a husky come-fuck-me voice says, "Honey, would you like some of this?"

The husband looks between his aging wife's legs, lets out his breath, looks up at his doting wife and replies, "Hell, no! Look what it's done to your underwear."

* * *

When should you steer clear of a redhead?
When she is out of batteries.

* * *

What is the difference between a bitch and redhead?
Not a damn thing, but you better not tell her that.

* * *

How many men does it take to please a redhead?
How many you got?

* * *

A lawyer married a redhead who had previously divorced ten husbands. On their wedding night, she told her new husband, "Please be a bit gentle; I'm still a virgin."

"What?" said the puzzled groom. "How can that be if you've been married ten times? And besides, you're a redhead! I can't understand it."

"Well, husband #1 was a Sales Representative—he kept telling me how great it was going to be.

Husband #2 was in Software Services—he was never really sure how it was supposed to function, but he said he'd look into it and get back to me.

Husband #3 was from Field Services—he said everything checked out diagnostically but he just couldn't get the system up.

Husband #4 was in Telemarketing—even though he knew he had the order, he didn't know when he would be able to deliver.

Husband #5 was an Engineer—he understood the basic process but wanted three years to research, implement, and design a new state-of-the-art method.

Husband #6 was from Finance and Administration—he thought he knew how, but he wasn't sure whether it was his job or not.

Husband #7 was in Marketing—although he had a product, he was never sure how to position it.

Husband #8 was a psychiatrist—all he ever did was talk about it.

Husband #9 was a gynecologist—all he did was look at it.

Husband #10 was a stamp collector—all he ever did was . . . God, I miss him!

But now that I've married you, I'm really excited!"

"Good," said the husband, "but, why?"

"Duh; you're a lawyer. This time I know I'm gonna get screwed!"

✳ ✳ ✳

Two elderly ladies, one of them a redhead, are sitting on the front porch, doing nothing. The redhead turns to the other and asks, "Do you still get horny?"

The other replies, "Oh sure I do."

The redhead then asks, "What do you do about it?"

The second old lady replies, "I suck a lifesaver."

After a few moments, the redhead asks, "Who drives you to the beach?"

＊ ＊ ＊

A redhead had a high-school sweetheart and they went out together for four years. They enjoyed losing their virginity with each other in 10th grade. When they graduated, they wanted to both go to the same college, but the redhead was accepted to a college on the east coast, and the guy went to the west coast. They agreed to be faithful to each other and spend anytime they could together.

As time went on, the guy would call the girl and she would never be home, and when he wrote, she would take weeks to return the letters. Even when he e-mailed her, she took days to return his messages. Finally, she confessed to him that she wanted to date around. He didn't take this very well and increased his calls, letters, and e-mails trying to win back her love. Because she became annoyed, and now had a new boyfriend, she wanted to get him off her back.

So, this is what she did: she took a snapshot of her having sex with her new boyfriend and sent it to her old boyfriend with a note reading, "I found a new boyfriend, leave me alone." Well, needless to say, this guy was heartbroken but, even more so, was pissed. So, what he did next was awesome.

He wrote on the back of the photo the following, "Dear Mom and Dad, having a great time at college, please send more money!" and mailed the photo to her parents.

✳ ✳ ✳

What does a redhead, an anniversary, and a toilet have in common?
Men always miss them.

✳ ✳ ✳

A man is sitting on a train across from a busty redhead who's wearing a tiny miniskirt. Despite his efforts, he is unable to stop staring at the top of the redhead's thighs. To his delight, he realizes she has gone without underwear.

The redhead realizes he is staring and inquires, "Are you looking at my pussy?" "Yes, I'm sorry," replies the man and promises to avert his eyes.

"It's quite all right," replies the redhead, "It's very talented—watch this, I'll make it blow a kiss to you." Sure enough, the pussy blows him a kiss.

The man, who is getting really interested, asks what else the wonder pussy can do. "I can also make it wink," says the redhead. The man stares in amazement as the pussy winks at him. "Come and sit next to me," she suggests, patting the seat. The man moves over and she then says, "Would you like to stick a couple of fingers in?"

Stunned, the man replies, "Fuck me! Can it whistle as well?"

✳ ✳ ✳

An extraordinarily handsome man decides he had the God-given responsibility to marry the perfect woman so they could produce children beyond comparison. With that as his goal, he begins searching for the perfect woman. After a diligent, but fruitless, search up and down the East coast, he heads west. Soon he meets a farmer with three gorgeous daughters with flame-red hair that positively takes his breath away. So he explains his mission to the farmer, asking for permission to marry one of his daughters.

The farmer simply replies, "They're all lookin' to get married, so you came to the right place. Look them over and select the one you want."

So the man dates the first redheaded daughter. The next day the farmer asks the man's opinion.

"Well," says the man, "She's just a weeeeee bit, not that you can hardly notice, pigeon-toed."

The farmer nods and suggests the man date one of the other girls; so the man goes out with the second red-haired daughter.

The next day, the farmer again asks how things went.

"Well," the man replies, "She's just a weeeee bit, not that you can hardly tell, cross-eyed."

The farmer nods and suggests he date the third redheaded daughter to see if things might be better. So the man does as the farmer recommends.

The next morning the man rushes in exclaiming, "She's perfect, just perfect! She's the one I want to marry!" So they wed right away.

Nine Months later the baby is born. When the man visits the nursery he is horrified by what he sees: the baby is the ugliest, most pathetic human you can imagine. He rushes over to his father-in-law, the farmer, asking how such a thing could happen, considering the parents.

"Well," explains the farmer, "She was just a weeeee bit, not that you could hardly tell, pregnant when you met her."

* * *

Three housewives—a brunette, a blonde and a redhead—were sitting around the table talking, and the subject turned to their husbands.

The brunette said, "My husband just won't go to church with me, I think he's going to go to hell."

This led to more discussion and it was generally agreed that, for one reason or another, all the husbands were going to end up in hell.

The housewives then started speculating about themselves. The brunette said "I try to be good—I'm sure I'll make it to Heaven."

The blonde then said, "Well, I did this bad thing, so I know I won't make it."

Then they noticed that the redhead wasn't saying anything. They looked at her and said, "You're such a nice lady, surely you're going to Heaven?"

The redhead replied, "No, first thing in the morning, I'm going to buy me a ticket straight to hell!"

Shocked, the other two wanted to know why she'd do such a thing.

"Well, you don't expect me to live in a world without men, do you?

✳ ✳ ✳

How do you know when your redhead has forgiven you?
She stops washing your clothes in the toilet bowl.

✳ ✳ ✳

A redhead and her husband were celebrating their golden wedding anniversary. Their domestic tranquility had long been the talk of the town, so a local newspaper reporter asked them for the secret of their long and happy marriage.

"Well, it dates back to our honeymoon," explained the husband. "We visited the Grand Canyon and took a trip down to the bottom of the canyon by pack mule.

"We hadn't gone too far when my wife's mule stumbled. My wife quietly said 'That's once.' We proceeded a little farther when the mule stumbled again. Once again my wife quietly said, 'That's twice! We hadn't gone a half-mile more when the mule stumbled a third time. My wife promptly removed a revolver from her purse and shot the mule. I started to protest about her killing the mule when she looked at me and quietly said, 'That's once.'"

✳ ✳ ✳

A very attractive redhead goes up to the bar in a quiet rural pub. She gestures alluringly to the bartender, who comes over immediately. When he arrives, she seductively signals that he should bring his face closer to hers. When he does so, she begins to gently caress his full beard. "Are you the manager?" she asks, softly stroking his face with both hands.

"Actually, no," the man replies.

"Can you get him for me? I need to speak to him," she says, running her hands beyond his beard and into his hair.

"I'm afraid I can't," breathes the bartender. "Is there anything I can do?"

"Yes, there is. I need you to give him a message," she continues huskily, popping a couple of fingers into his mouth and allowing him to suck them gently.

"What should I tell him?" the bartender manages to say.

"Tell him," she whispers, "There is no toilet paper or hand soap in the ladies' room."

✳ ✳ ✳

How do you know a guy at the beach has a redhead for a girlfriend?
She has scratched "Stay Off My Turf!" on his back with her nails.

✳ ✳ ✳

There were two old men sitting on a park bench, when a pretty blonde walks by. One of the old men says to the other one, "Ever sleep with a blonde?"

The other old man says wistfully, "Many a time. Many a time."

Before long, an attractive brunette walks by. The old man again says to the other, "Ever sleep with a brunette?"

Shrugging, the other old man replies, "Many a time. Many a time."

A leggy redhead then walks by, and the old man asks the other, "Ever sleep with a redhead?"

Grinning, the other old man says, "Not a wink."

* * *

A male pastor walked into a neighborhood pub to use the restroom. The place was lively with music and dancing, until people saw the pastor. As the room suddenly became quiet, he walked up to the redhead bartender and asked her, "May I please use the restroom?"

The redhead replied, "I really don't think you should."

"Why not?" the pastor asked. "I really need to use a restroom!"

"Well, I don't think you should. There is a statue of a naked woman in there and she's only covered by a fig leaf!"

"Nonsense," said the pastor, "I'll look the other way!"

So the bartender showed the clergyman the door at the top of the stairs, and he proceeded to the restroom. After a few minutes he came back out, and the whole place was filled with music and dancing again. The pastor went up to the bartender and said, "Miss, I, don't understand. When I came in here, the place was hopping with music and dancing. Then the room became absolutely quiet. I went to the restroom, and now the place is hopping again."

"Well, now you're one of us!" said the redhead. "Would you like a drink too?"

"But, I still don't understand," said the puzzled pastor.

"You see," laughed the redhead, "every time the fig leaf is lifted on the statue, the lights go out in the whole place. Now, how about that drink?"

✳ ✳ ✳

"Marrying a redhead is like a phone call in the night: first the ring, and then you wake up.

✳ ✳ ✳

Right in the middle of lovemaking, the husband of a redhead dies of a heart attack. As the funeral arrangements are being made, the mortician informs the widow that he cannot get rid of her dead husband's rigor mortis hard-on, which is sticking straight up in the air, and if they don't do something, it will look odd in the coffin at the funeral.

The redhead tells the guy to cut it off and stick it up her dear departed's behind. The mortician can't believe his ears, but the widow is adamant, so he does it. During the funeral, friends and relatives of the dead man are concerned to see a tear in the corner of his eye, but the widow assures them that there is no cause for alarm.

Just before the casket is closed, the widow leans in and whispers in the dead man's ear, "It hurts, doesn't it?"

* * *

Differences between Brunettes and Redheads:

Brunettes never go after another girl's man.
Redheads go after him and his brother.

Brunettes wear white cotton panties.
Redheads don't wear any.

Brunettes never consider sleeping with the boss.
Redheads never do either, unless he's very, very rich.

Brunettes prefer the missionary position.
Redheads do too—when acting out a "virgin" fantasy.

Brunettes wear high heels to work.
Redheads wear high heels to bed.

Brunettes have stocks.
Redheads have stockbrokers.

Brunettes collect silk shirts.
Redheads collect silk teddies.

Brunettes just say "No."
Redheads just say "When?"

Brunettes never do "it" on the first date.
Redheads wait to see what kind of car
    he's driving.

Brunettes read best-sellers.
Redheads sleep with the authors.

Brunettes write condolence notes.
Redheads marry the widower.

Brunettes loosen a few buttons when it's hot.
Redheads make it hot by loosening a
    few buttons.

Brunettes wax their floors.
Redheads wax their bikini lines.

Brunettes blush during sex scenes in a movie.
Redheads know they could do it better.

Brunettes think they're not fully dressed without
a strand of pearls.
Redheads think they're fully dressed with just a
strand of pearls.

Brunettes only own one credit card and rarely
use it.
Redheads only own one bra and rarely use it.

Brunettes pack their toothbrush.
Redheads pack their diaphragms.

Brunettes think the office is the wrong place to
have sex.
Redheads think no place is the wrong place to
have sex.

Brunettes prefer the missionary position.
Redheads do, too, but only for starters.

Brunettes say "Thanks for a wonderful dinner."
Redheads say, "What's for breakfast?"

Brunettes keep a diary.
Redheads don't have time to keep a diary.

Brunettes love Italian food.
Redheads love Italian waiters.

Brunettes will apologize and kiss your ass.
Redheads will never apologize, but tell you to
"Kiss my lily-white ass."

✳ ✳ ✳

A redheaded woman came home just in time to
find her husband in bed with another woman. With
superhuman strength borne of fury, she dragged
her husband down the stairs to the garage and put
his penis in a vise. She then secured it tightly and
removed the handle. Next she picked up a hacksaw.

The terrified husband screamed, "STOP!!
STOP!! You're NOT going to cut it off, ARE YOU?"

The wife, with a gleam of revenge in her eye,
laid down the hacksaw within her husbands reach
and said "Nope. I'm going to set the garage on fire."

✳ ✳ ✳

A redhead is just a blonde who didn't make
the finals.

✳ ✳ ✳

Upon entering the confessional, a young redhead spilled the beans, admitting: "Last night my boyfriend made mad passionate love to me—seven times."

The priest thought long and hard, then said, "Take seven lemons and squeeze them into a glass, then drink it."

The young woman asked, "Will this cleanse me of my sins?"

The priest said, "No, but it will wipe the smile off your face."

* * *

Why do redheads pay more attention to their appearance than improving their minds?
Because most men are stupid, but few are blind.

* * *

A redhead went out with a guy who said, "I'm going to make love to you like you've never been made love to before."

A half-hour later, the redhead plucked a feather from the pillow and stroked the guy's head.

He asked, "What the heck are you doing?"

The redhead replied, "Comparatively speaking, I'm beating your brains out."

✳ ✳ ✳

What's the difference between a dog howling on the back porch, and a redhead howling on the front porch?
The dog shuts up when you let it in.

✳ ✳ ✳

What do redheads and razor-wire have in common?
Handle both with care.

✳ ✳ ✳

Seen inscribed on a tombstone: "Beneath this stone lies the guy who told that last bad redhead joke."

✳ ✳ ✳

You may sleep with a blonde and you may sleep with a brunette, but you will never sleep with a redhead.

✳ ✳ ✳

Redheads are just blondes with high blood pressure.

* * *

Why do guys date blondes?
All the redheads are taken.

* * *

Three roommates—a blonde, a brunette, and a redhead—all go out on dates one night. When they get back in, the blonde says, "You know you've been on a good date when your make-up is all smeared!" The brunette says, "No, you know you've been on a good date when you come home and your hair is all messed up." The redhead doesn't say anything, she just reaches up under her skirt, pulls off her panties, and throws them against the wall.

* * *

Three nurses—a blonde, a brunette, and a redhead—all decided to play jokes on the handsome young doctor they worked for. Later that day, they all got together on their break and discussed what they had each done to the doctor. The blonde nurse said, "I put cotton in his stethoscope so he couldn't hear." The brunette nurse said, "Well, I did something much worse than that. I poked holes in all his condoms." The redhead nurse fainted.

＊ ＊ ＊

Two bored casino dealers are waiting at a craps table.

A very attractive redhead comes in and wants to bet twenty thousand dollars on a single roll of the dice.

She says, "I hope you don't mind, but I feel much luckier when I'm bottomless."

With that, she strips naked from the waist down, and rolls the dice while yelling, "Momma needs a new pair of pants!"

The redhead then begins jumping up and down, hugging each of the dealers. "I win! I win!" She then picks up her money and clothes and quickly leaves. The dealers just stare at each other dumbfounded.

Finally, one of them asks the other, "What did she roll anyway?"

The other answers, "I thought you were watching!"

* * *

A redhead called the police department and reported that she had been assaulted. The officer who answered the phone asked, "When did this happen?"

She replied, "Last week."

The police officer then asked, "Why did you wait until now to report it?"

"Well," she said. "I didn't know that I was assaulted until the check bounced."

* * *

A guy with a hot redheaded wife was talking to his buddy at the bar and saying, "I don't know what to get my wife for her birthday—she has everything, and besides, she can afford to buy anything she wants, so I'm stumped." His buddy says, "I have an idea—why don't you make up a certificate saying she can have sixty minutes of great sex, any way she wants it—she'll probably be thrilled." So that's what the husband did.

The next day at the bar his buddy asks the guy, "Well? Did you take my suggestion?"

"Yes, I did," replies the husband.

"Did she like it?" his buddy asks, smiling.

"Oh yeah." says the husband, looking surprisingly forlorn. "She jumped up, thanked me, kissed me on the forehead, and ran out the door, yelling, "I'll be back in an hour!"

* * *

The Devil walks into a crowded bar. Within seconds, the bar empties, with people running out screaming all over the place, all except for one older redheaded lady leaning over the bar. The Devil wanders across to the redheaded woman and says, "Do you know who I am?"

The woman takes a sip of his beer, then answers, "Yep."

The Devil stares at the old redhead and asks, "Well, aren't you afraid of me?"

She looks the Devil up and down for a minute then shrugs, "I married your brother twenty-five years ago, so why the hell should I be scared of you?"

* * *

Redheads are like a well-trained dog.
Make a move and they roll over and play dead.

* * *

How do you know if a guy has a redheaded secretary?
He's always smiling.

* * *

1st guy: "I'm a man of few words."
    2nd guy: "I married a redhead, too."

* * *

A doctor had been married to a redhead for ten years. One day he told her, "You need to do something to spice up our lovemaking." Shortly thereafter, he came home and found her in bed with another man, who was also a doctor.

"Why?" asked the redhead's husband.

The redhead wife replies, "You said I needed to do something to spice up our lovemaking; I just wanted to get a second opinion."

* * *

A red-haired new bride moved into the small home on her husband's ranch. She put a shoebox on a shelf in her closet and asked her husband never to touch it. For fifty years her husband left the box alone until the redhead was old and dying. One day when he was putting their affairs in order, he found the box again and thought it might hold something important. Opening it, he found two doilies and $82,500 in cash.

He took the box to his wife and asked about the contents.

"My mother gave me that box the day we married," she explained. "She told me never to start a fight or let my redheaded temper get the better of me. She said to make a doily to help ease my frustrations every time I got mad at you."

The husband was very touched that in fifty years she'd only been mad at him twice.

"What's the $82,500 for?" he asked.

"Oh, that's the money I made selling the rest of the doilies."

* * *

A small tourist hotel was all abuzz about an afternoon wedding where the groom was ninety-five and the bride was a vivacious redheaded gold digger of twenty-three. The groom looked pretty feeble and the feeling was that the wedding night might kill him, because his bride was a healthy and energetic young woman.

But, lo and behold, the next morning the redhead came down the main staircase slowly, one step at a time, hanging on to the banister for dear life.

She finally managed to get to the counter of the little shop in the hotel. The clerk looked really concerned and asked the young bride, "Whatever happened to you, honey? You look like you've been wrestling an alligator!"

The bride groaned, hung on to the counter and managed to speak,

"Oh God! My husband told me he'd been saving up for seventy-five years, and I thought he meant his money!"

✳ ✳ ✳

A redheaded wife found out that her husband a military man, was cheating on her while stationed in Germany. So she sends him this care package. He is excited to get a package from his wife back home and finds that it contains a batch of homemade cookies and a DVD of his favorite TV shows. He invites a couple of his buddies over and they're all sitting around having a great time eating the cookies and watching some episodes of *South Park*.

Right in the middle of one episode, the program cuts to a home video of his wife on her knees sucking his best friend's cock. After a few seconds, the friend blows his load in her pie hole, and she turns and spits the load right into the mixing bowl of cookie dough. She then looks at the camera and says, "By the way, I want a divorce."

✳ ✳ ✳

A blonde, a brunette and a redhead are at the doctor's office.

The blonde goes in to see the doctor. When the doctor examines her, he notices a big Y on her chest. The doctor asks, "Why do you have a big Y on your chest?"

She replies, "Well, my boyfriend went to Yale, and when we make love he likes to wear his college sweater."

The doctor nods and next sees the brunette patient. When he examines her, he notices a big H on her chest. Again, the doctor asks, "How did you get a big H on your chest?"

The brunette replies, "My husband went to Harvard and when we make love he likes to wear his college sweater."

The doctor just nods his head and continues on with the redhead. As he examines her, he notices once again that this woman also has a letter on her chest. This time it's a large M. He says, "Don't tell me, your boyfriend went to Michigan?"

"No," replies the redhead. "But my girlfriend went to Wisconsin."

✳ ✳ ✳

It's easy to get the ride of your life. First, seduce a redhead. Mount her from behind, start going nice and slow, taking her hair in your hand. Then pull her head back slightly and whisper in her ear, "Your sister was better than you . . ." and try to hold on for eight seconds!

✳ ✳ ✳

What a Redhead Really Means When:

A redhead says: You want.
A redhead means: You want.

A redhead says: We need.
A redhead means: I want.

A redhead says: It's your decision.
A redhead means: The correct decision should be obvious.

A redhead says: Do what you want.
A redhead means: You'll pay for this later.

A redhead says: We need to talk.
A redhead means: I need to complain.

A redhead says: Sure . . . go ahead.
A redhead means: You better not.

A redhead says: I'm not upset.
A redhead means: Of course I'm upset, you moron!

A redhead says: You're so manly.
A redhead means: You sweat a lot and need a shave.

A redhead says: Be romantic, turn out the lights.
A redhead means: I have flabby thighs.

A redhead says: This kitchen is so outdated.
A redhead means: I want a new house.

A redhead says: I want new curtains.
A redhead means: And carpeting, furniture,
    and wallpaper!

A redhead says: I need wedding shoes.
A redhead means: The other forty pairs are the
    wrong shade of white.

A redhead says: Hang the picture there.
A redhead means: No, I mean hang it there!

A redhead says: I heard a noise.
A redhead means: I noticed you were almost
    asleep.

A redhead says: Do you love me?

A redhead means: I'm going to ask for something expensive.

A redhead says: How much do you love me?

A redhead means: I did something today you're not going to like.

A redhead says: I'll be ready in a minute.

A redhead means: Kick off your shoes and take an hour nap.

A redhead says: Am I fat?

A redhead means: Tell me I'm beautiful.

A redhead says: You have to learn to communicate.

A redhead means: Just agree with me.

A redhead says: Are you listening to me?

A redhead means: Too late, you're doomed.

A redhead says: Yes.

A redhead means: No.

A redhead says: No.

A redhead means: No.

A redhead says: Maybe.

A redhead means: No.

A redhead says: I'm sorry.

A redhead means: You'll be sorry.

A redhead says: Do you like this recipe?

A redhead means: You better get used to it.

A redhead says: All I'm going to buy is a soap dish.

A redhead means: I'm coming back with enough to fill this place.

A redhead says: Was that the baby?

A redhead means: Get out of bed and check on the baby.

A redhead says: I'm not yelling!

A redhead means: Yes I am! This is important!

✳ ✳ ✳

In answer to the question "What's wrong?"

A redhead says: The same old thing.

A redhead means: Nothing.

A redhead says: Nothing.

A redhead means: Everything.

A redhead says: Nothing, really.

A redhead means: It's just that you're an idiot.

A redhead says: I don't want to talk about it.

A redhead means: I'm still building up steam.

✳ ✳ ✳

Top 17 Things Not to Say to a Pregnant Redhead:

17. "I finished the Oreos."

16. "Not to imply anything, but I don't think the kid weighs forty pounds."

15. "Y'know, looking at her, you'd never guess that Angelina Jolie had a baby."

14. "I sure hope your thighs aren't going to stay that flabby forever."

13. "Well, couldn't they induce labor? The 25th is the Super Bowl."

12. "Darned if you aren't about five pounds away from a surprise visit from that Richard Simmons fella."

11. "Fred at the office passed a stone the size of a pea. Boy, that's gotta hurt."

10. "Whoa! For a minute there, I thought I woke up next to The Goodyear Blimp!"

9. "I'm jealous. Why can't men experience the joy of childbirth?"

8. "Are your ankles supposed to look like that?"

7. "Get your own ice cream."

6. "Geez, you're awfully puffy-looking today."

5. "Got milk?"

4. "Maybe we should name the baby after my secretary, Tawney."

3. "Man! That rose tattoo on your hip is the size of Madagascar!"

2. "Retaining water? Yeah, like the Hoover Dam retains water."

1. And the number one thing not to say if a redhead is pregnant is, "You don't have the guts to pull that trigger."

Other Ulysses Press Books

The Dirtiest, Most Politically Incorrect Jokes Ever
Allan Pease, $12.95
This book is packed with no-holds-barred gags for those who are fed up with others telling them what to say, how to think, and what is allowed to be funny.

The Big Ass Book of Jokes
Rudy A. Swale, $14.95
The thousands of jokes in this huge volume range from clean enough to tell at work to too off-color for corporate e-mail.

Blonde Walks into a Bar: The 4,000 Most Hilarious, Gut-Busting Gags, One-Liners and Jokes
Jonathan Swan, $14.95
Unapologetically funny and irreverent, this book holds nothing back as it delivers laugh after laugh.

The Ginormous Book of Dirty Jokes: Over 1000 Sick, Filthy and X-Rated Jokes
Rudy A. Swale, $12.95
This masterpeice offers the biggest, baddest, badassest collection of off-color quips.

The Girl's-Only Dirty Joke Book
Karen S. Smith, $10.95
From under-sized penises and unfaithful men to over-sized breasts and less-than-brilliant blondes, this book serves up the filthiest female humor ever put into print.

Man Walks into a Bar: Over 6,000 of the Most Hilarious Jokes, Funniest Insults and Gut-Busting One-Liners

Stephen Arnott & Mike Haskins, $14.95

This book is packed full of quick and easy jokes that are as simple to remember and repeat as they are funny.

The Sassy Bitch's Book of Dirty Jokes

Katie Reynolds, $10.95

This joke book features outrageous one-liners, stories, and punch lines on everything from romance, one-nighters and dirty talk to foreplay, penis size, and between-the-sheets mishaps.

Seriously Sick Jokes: The Most Disgusting, Filthy, Offensive Jokes from the Vile, Obscene, Disturbed Minds of b3ta.com

Compiled by Rob Manuel, $10.95

Seriously Sick Jokes is a lewd, crude, and absolutely filthy collection that will have readers cringing between bouts of uncontrollable laughter.

The Ultimate Dirty Joke Book

Mike Oxbent & Harry P. Ness, $11.95

This joke collection holds back nothing and guarantees outrageous laughs.

To order these books call 800-377-2542 or 510-601-8301, fax 510-601-8307, e-mail ulysses@ulyssespress.com, or write to Ulysses Press, P.O. Box 3440, Berkeley, CA 94703. All retail orders are shipped free of charge. California residents must include sales tax. Allow two to three weeks for delivery.

About the Author

James Buffington has been collecting humor for over 30 years. He has a wife, Gail, and three kids, two of whom are autistic. His goal is to build future income for the kids when he is no longer able to care for them. Currently, he operates the popular gift and T-shirt website, www.politicsisfun.com, and the blog, www.dailyobamajokes.com. Jim and his family also have two cats, Callie and The Grey, who attend to all the family's spiritual needs.